Module 1

The Challenge of Learning to Read

Language Essentials for Teachers of Reading and Spelling

Louisa C. Moats, Ed.D.

SOPRIS WEST™ EDUCATIONAL SERVICES
A CAMBIUM LEARNING COMPANY

BOSTON, MA • LONGMONT, CO

08 07 06 05 8 7 6 5

ISBN 1-59318-189-2

Printed in the United States of America

Published and Distributed by

SOPRIS
WEST™
EDUCATIONAL SERVICES

A Cambium Learning™ Company

4093 Specialty Place • Longmont, CO 80504 • (303) 651-2829
www.sopriswest.com

191MOD1/11-05

Dedication

To my husband, Steve Mitchell, whose support is constant and invaluable.

Acknowledgments

The LETRS modules have been developed with the help of many people. Our active national trainers, including Carol Tolman, Susan Hall, Marcia Davidson, Anne Cunningham, Marcia Berger, Deb Glaser, Linda Farrell, Judi Dodson, and Anne Whitney have all offered valuable suggestions for improving the module content and structure. Their devotion to delivering LETRS across the country is appreciated beyond measure. Bruce Rosow, Kevin Feldman, Susan Lowell, Patricia Mathes, Marianne Steverson, Lynn Kuhn, Jan Hasbrouck, and Nancy Eberhardt contributed their expertise to the first edition and continue to provide essential input and feedback. Many other professionals from all over the country who have attended institutes and offered constructive criticism have enabled our response to educators. I hope you see your ideas reflected in the revised editions of this continually evolving material.

I am grateful for the daily support and energy of the Sopris West office staff, editors, and designers including Lynne Stair, Sue Campbell, Sandra Knauke, Christine Kosmicki, and Kim Harris. Special thanks are due to Toni Backstrom, who manages the LETRS program with enthusiasm, competence, and commitment.

Stu Horsfall, Ray Beck, Steve Mitchell, Chet Foraker, and Steve Kukic are the vision and energy behind the publication of evidence-based programs in education that will help all children learn. I am so fortunate to be working with all of you.

—LCM

Contents for Module 1

Overview 1

Content of LETRS Modules Within the Language-Literacy Connection 3

Self-Evaluation 3

Objectives 5

Why Reading Instruction is a National Priority 6

Key Vocabulary 9

Learning to Read is Not Natural 10
- Exercise #1: Reading Problems in Your School 10
- Learning to Read is Not Like Learning to Talk 11
- Spoken and Written Language Differ 12
  - Exercise #2: Comparison of Spoken and Written Language 13
- What's Special About An Alphabet? 15
  - Exercise #3: Reflections on Writing Systems 16
- Awareness of Speech Sounds and the Alphabetic Principle 16
  - Exercise #4: Simulation of Learning to Read 19

What the Mind Does When It Reads 20
- Eye Movements and Reading 22
- Four Processing Systems 23
- What About Cueing Systems? 28
  - Exercise #5: Which Processors are Involved? 29

How Children Learn to Read 30
- The Continuum of Reading Development 30
- A Description of Reading "Stages" 31
- Phases of Word Reading Development 33
- Case Study Examples of Early Reading and Spelling Development 35
- Achieving Passage Reading Fluency With Comprehension 40
  - Exercise #6: Describe the Child's Phase of Reading Development 42

Components of Comprehensive Reading Instruction 44
- Components Typically Emphasized at Each Grade Level 45
  - Exercise #7: Identify What Component is Addressed 46

Dyslexia and Other Causes of Reading Failure 47
- What About Dyslexia? 47
  - Exercise #8: Discussion of Work Samples From Children With Reading Problems 51

Summary 54
- Exercise #9: Concluding Reflections 55

Bibliography 56

Teacher Participant Pages—Exercise #4 59

Glossary 67

Appendix A 73
- Answers to Applicable Exercises

Appendix B 77
- Exercise #4: Learning to Read With Novel Symbols: Guide for the Module Instructor

Overview of LETRS: Language Essentials for Teachers of Reading and Spelling

LETRS is designed to enrich and extend, but not to replace, program-specific professional development for teachers of reading and language arts. Teachers who implement a core, comprehensive reading program must know the format and instructional routines necessary to implement daily lessons. Teaching reading is complex and demanding, and new teachers will need both modeling and classroom coaching to implement the program well. Program-specific training, however, is not enough to enable teachers to tailor instruction to the diverse needs in their classrooms. Even teachers who are getting good results will need to understand the research-based principles of reading development, reading differences, and reading instruction. Reaching *all* learners through assessment and intervention is only possible when the teacher understands who is having difficulty, why they might be struggling, and what approaches to intervention are grounded in evidence. An empowered teacher is one who knows and can implement the best practices of the field, as established by a scientific research consensus.

The American Federation of Teachers' *Teaching Reading Is Rocket Science* and the Learning First Alliance's *Every Child Reading: A Professional Development Guide* provided the blueprint for these modules. LETRS modules teach concepts about language structure, reading development, reading difficulty, and assessment practices that guide research-based instruction. The format of instruction in LETRS allows for deep learning and reflection beyond the brief "once over" treatment the topics are typically given. Our professional development approach has been successful with diverse groups of teachers: regular classroom and special education, novice and expert, rural and urban.

The modules address each component of reading instruction in depth—phonological and phonemic awareness; phonics, decoding, spelling, and word study; oral language development; vocabulary; reading fluency; comprehension; and writing—as well as the links among these components. The characteristics and the needs of second language learners (ELL), dialect speakers, and students with other learning differences are woven into the modules. Assessment modules teach a problem-solving strategy for grouping children and designing instruction.

Teachers usually need extended time to learn and apply the knowledge and skills included in LETRS, depending on their background and experience. The content is dense by design. Each module is written so that teacher participants will engage in questions, problems, and tasks that lead to understanding, but understanding may occur in small steps, gradually, over several years. Some of the modules also are accompanied by the LETRS Interactive CD-ROMS, self-instructional supplements for independent study and practice, developed with the help of a grant from the SBIR program of the National Institute for Child Health and Human Development.

More information about LETRS material, programs, and institutes is available at www.letrs.com.

Content of LETRS Modules Within the Language-Literacy Connection

Components of Comprehensive Reading Instruction	Organization of Language						
	Phonology	Morphology	Orthography	Semantics	Syntax	Discourse and Pragmatics	Etymology
Phonological Awareness	2	2					
Phonics, Spelling, and Word Study	3, 7	3, 7, 10	3, 7, 10				3, 10
Fluency	5		5	5	5		
Vocabulary	4	4	4	4	4		4
Text Comprehension		6		6	6	6, 11	
Written Expression			9, 11	9, 11	9, 11	9, 11	
Assessment	8, 12	8, 12	8, 12	8, 12	8, 12	8, 12	

Self-Evaluation

1. Rate your knowledge of each of the following vocabulary terms. Rate the word as:
   (1) Unknown if the term is completely unfamiliar.
   (2) Acquainted if a basic meaning is recognized after some thought.
   (3) Established if meaning is easily, rapidly, and automatically recognized and you feel you can explain it to others.

   1 = Unknown   2 = Acquainted   3 = Established

1 alphabetic principle	3 chunk
3 context	2 dyslexia
1 grapheme	1 logographic
1 morpheme	2 orthography
2 phoneme	2 phonological processing
2 phonological awareness	1 rapid automatic naming
1 semantics	3 syllable

2. Response to Children's Writing

After looking at the writing samples below, answer these questions:

(a) Is the kindergarten child on track for reading success? Why?

(b) What do spellings such as "jragd" for "dragged," "gobrigh" for "drawbridge," and "hows" for "house" mean about the child's future ability to read and spell?

(c) The second grader's sentence was all he wrote during a 20-minute composition on making breakfast for a friend. What does that suggest about the child's language characteristics?

(d) The fourth grader has great difficulty writing the grammatical endings on words. What could account for that problem?

(e) What kind of instruction is likely to help the fourth grader use standard word forms and word order in writing?

Then the witch came off her broomstc. Then the witch went ovr the gobrigh [drawbridge). Than the witch noct on the door then the princess opind the door then the witch grab the princess and then the witct jragd that princess to her hows. Then a prince so the witch jragen the princss to her hows. Then the prince went aftr the witch bat the prince was to fat. Then the naxt dai the witch jragd the princss to a hi op towr with no stars no dor.

—May of kindergarten

Sometime you can make pancakes with agg and with mike and you can make pancakes with buttr and grise.

—End of second grade

I was also frighten when i was going home and i was by lots of trees and it was lighting. I was so frightened my that. Sometime thing could be so frightened that you could junp out of your shoes. Things that are frightingly can scare you that you will not no what happen to you. I hate frighened things.

—End of fourth grade

Objectives

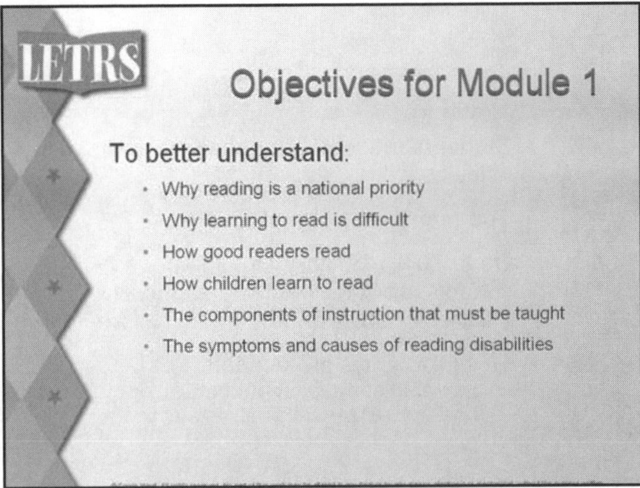

Slide 1

- Summarize why the teaching of reading has become a national priority.
- Understand why learning to read is difficult for many students.
  - List some major differences between spoken and written language.
  - Explain the unique demands of alphabetic writing.
  - Experience a "learning to read" exercise using a novel alphabet.
- Develop awareness of what the mind does when it reads—how good readers read.
  - Become familiar with the four-processor model of reading.
  - Understand that reading depends on language proficiency.
- With examples of student work, explore the progression of reading development—how children learn to read.
- Recognize tasks that are typical of each component of comprehensive reading instruction.
- Understand that biological, genetic, cognitive, environmental, and instructional causes interact to influence reading development.
- Review the characteristics of dyslexia.

Why Reading Instruction Is a National Priority

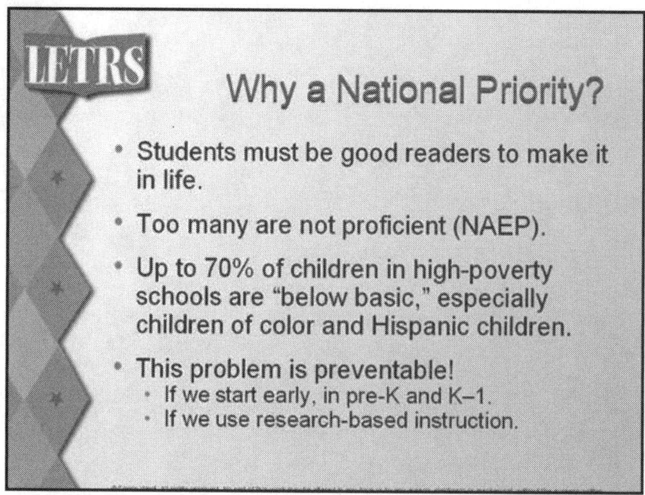

Slide 2

National concern about the quality of our schools and the achievement of all students is as high as it has ever been. The National Institute of Child Health and Human Development (NICHD) has characterized reading difficulty as a major public health concern because reading failure is associated with social ills such as dropping out of school, delinquency, unwanted pregnancy, and chronic underemployment. Poor reading affects about 38% of fourth grade students nationally, according to the most recent National Assessment of Educational Progress (NAEP), and up to 70% of poor students, especially African American, Hispanic, and Native American children who live in urban or isolated areas. Unless children learn to read well, they cannot make it in twenty-first-century society.

The good news is that the devastating educational and social consequences that stem from reading failure can be prevented. Several recent summaries of reading research[1] agree that all but 2 to 5% of children can learn to read, even in populations where the incidence of poor reading is often far higher. Students' success, however, depends on whether their teachers use sound, proven, effective programs and practices, and whether those practices are implemented with sufficient skill and intensity.

Citing over 30 years of research on reading, the United States Congress recently funded a substantial investment in early identification and prevention of reading problems called the Reading First initiative. Associated with the emphasis on early intervention is also a move to change intervention practices so that students with difficulties will be caught early before they fall too far behind. The insistence of policymakers that every child has the right to learn to read is based on a large body of scientific evidence indicating that we can find children before they fail and ensure their success in this most fundamental skill. The goal to "leave

[1] Adams, 1990; Snow, Burns, & Griffin, 1998; Fletcher & Lyon, 1998; Pressley, 1998; National Institute of Child Health and Human Development, 2000.

no child behind," however, can be achieved only if teacher preparation and professional development in reading education is upgraded to incorporate the findings from decades of research.

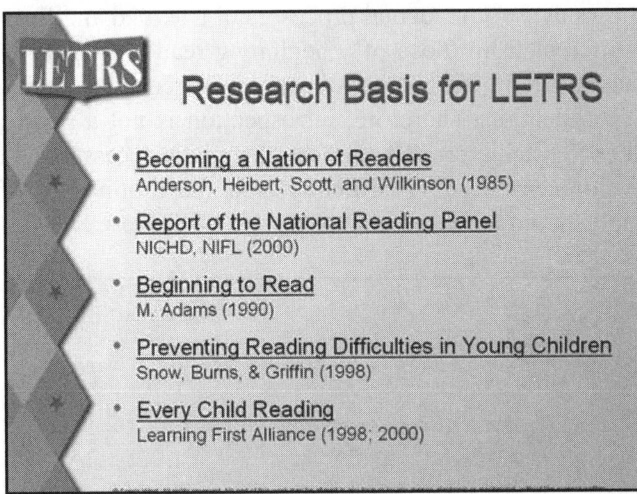

Slide 3

Discussion Question: When you hear the term "research based," what does that mean to you? Have you been able to read any of the research consensus documents?

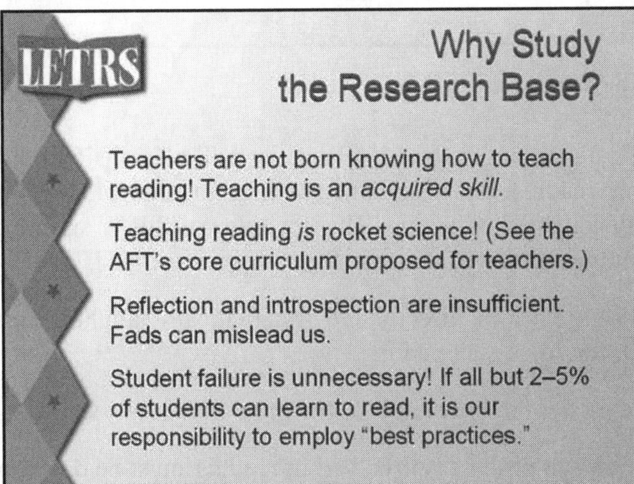

Slide 4

Research findings on how children learn to read, why some children fail, and the components and practices of effective instruction need to be applied on a widespread, consistent basis. Yet, faced with a struggling reader, many teachers feel unsure and question what to do. There is a need to disseminate research findings about reading so that every teacher will be able to help the poor readers in their classes. Findings from the National Reading Panel and other consensus documents give us a blueprint for effective instruction.

www.aft.org/edissues/rocketscience.htm

What makes an expert reading teacher?
- not all kids learn the same way
- some kids learn faster than others
- good readers know how to manipulate sounds
- good readers read frequently - practice, practice, practice

Adults who teach reading may remember that learning to read was, for them, easy and perhaps effortless. Because of this, they may have trouble understanding why reading is difficult for so many children. Not only may they have forgotten *how* they learned, but also they may have had aptitudes and opportunities that distinguished them from many children in their classes.

Research shows us that the mental processes of a skilled and fluent adult reader are different from those of a beginning reader. Mental activities critical to fluent reading are not consciously experienced or easily accessible through reflection. Therefore, introspection is not a good teacher when it comes to teaching reading. In short, study is necessary—study of reading development, reading difficulty, and the routines of effective teaching—and should be based on our best scientific research.

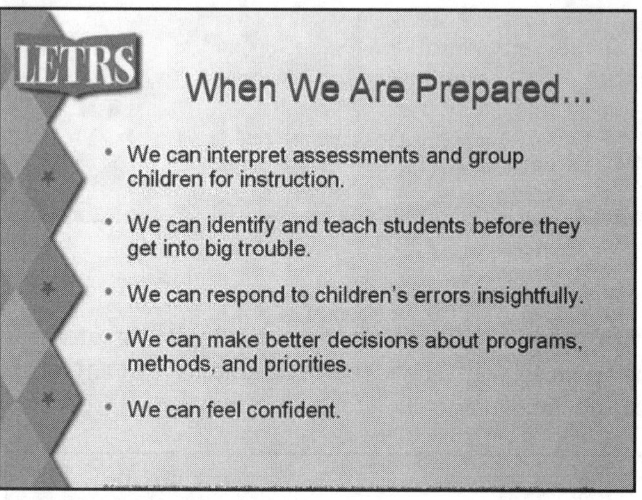

Slide 5

Combined, the modules in the LETRS series will offer insights and skills for teaching reading, spelling, and writing to students who require informed, systematic instruction. This module will foster six introductory understandings that will underlie the remainder of LETRS:

1. Reading must be directly and systematically taught for many children to be successful.
2. The earlier the intervention, the more likely its success.
3. All mental processes involved in reading must be developed, separately and together, including sound processing, print processing, knowledge of word meanings, and knowledge of the language in books.
4. Instruction should be tailored to each student's stage of reading development.
5. If teachers teach all components of a comprehensive lesson using informed, validated approaches, most children will learn to read, spell, and write.
6. Most children with reading disabilities or low reading achievement can be taught to read.

Key Vocabulary for Module 1

[From the Glossary in the back of the book]

alphabetic principle: (appreciation of) the correspondence of letters and letter combinations (graphemes) to phonemes

chunk: a group of letters that is processed as a unit corresponding to a piece of a word, usually a consonant cluster, onset-rime pattern, syllable, or morpheme

context: the language that surrounds a given word or phrase (linguistic context), or the field of meaningful associations that surrounds a given word or phrase (experiential context)

dyslexia: an impairment of reading accuracy and fluency attributable to an underlying phonological deficit (see the complete definition later in this module)

grapheme: a letter or letter combination that spells a phoneme; it may be one, two, three, or four letters in English (*e*, *ei*, *igh*, *eigh*)

logographic: a form of writing that represents the meaning of words and concepts with pictures or signs; contrasts with writing systems that represent speech sounds

morpheme: the smallest meaningful unit in language; it may be a word or part of a word; it may be one or more syllables, as in *un-inter-rupt-able*

orthography: the writing system of a language

phoneme: one of the speech sound units that is combined to make words in a language; English has 40 to 44 phonemes

phonological processing: perception, memory, retrieval, and pronunciation of the speech sound system, including stress patterns; the base layer of language processing

phonology: the rule system within a language by which its phonemes can be sequenced, combined, and pronounced

semantics: the study of systems of word meanings and relationships

syllable: the unit of oral language pronunciation that is organized around a vowel; it may or may not have consonants before or after the vowel

Learning to Read Is Not Natural[2]

Exercise #1: Reading Problems in Your School

What is your view of the reading problems prevalent in your school, district, or state? (5–10 minutes of discussion)

a. What is the typical "poor reader" like in your class, school, or district?

____

b. About what percentage of children are known to have trouble in your setting, and by what criterion are they identified?

____

c. Does there seem to be one major cause of reading difficulty or a combination of causes that interact with one another?

____

d. Do you think it is important to understand the cause of a reading problem in order to treat it?

____

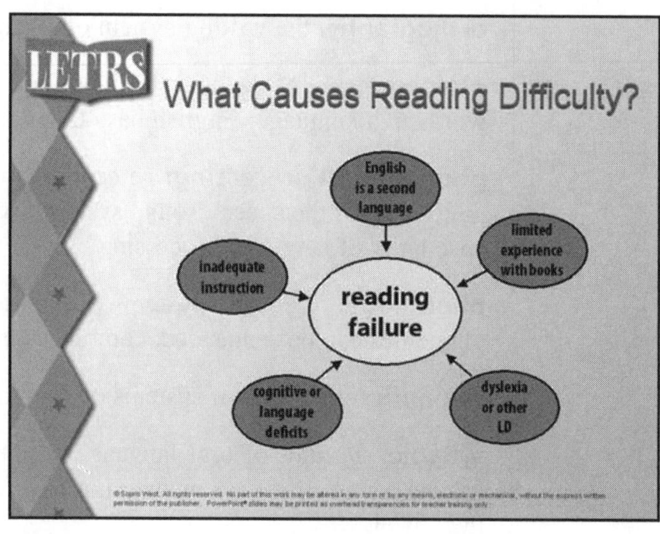

Slide 6

2 See Liberman, 1999.

Learning to Read Is Not Like Learning to Talk

Evidence That Alphabetic Reading Is Not "Natural"

- Alphabetic reading is a relatively new human capability, invented about 3500 B.C.
- We're not biologically "wired" to read and write as we are for oral language.
- Many people don't learn: 25% of the adult population of the U.S. has not learned to read.
- A child learns to speak at age one; reading is learned beginning at age five or six, and takes several years.

Slide 7

Spoken language is hard-wired in the human brain. It is difficult to prevent any hearing child from learning to speak if he or she hears language from caregivers. By the time a child is ten months of age, he or she has already learned how to recognize the speech sounds or phonemes of his or her caretakers' language and has lost some of the capacity to distinguish and produce the phonemes of other languages (Kuhl et al., 1992).

Language comprehension is substantial even within the first year of life, and most children use their biological aptitude for learning grammar to generate simple sentences by the time they are sixteen to twenty-four months of age. The few children known to scientists who did not learn to speak in early childhood, such as the Wild Boy of Aveyron and the closet child, Genie,[3] were almost totally isolated from other people during their critical early years.

A related fact should be self-evident: Reading and writing are acquired skills for which the human brain is not yet fully evolved. With teaching, children typically learn to read at about age five or six and need several years to master the skill. Sophisticated reading comprehension is the goal of eight to sixteen more years of schooling.

In the United States, the government estimates that 25% of the adult population cannot read with the fluency, accuracy, and comprehension necessary to read labels, newspapers, schedules, or manuals. One out of four individuals is said to be functionally illiterate. Obviously, these individuals do not learn to read better just because they are exposed to print in the environment. The myth, perpetuated as fact, that people learn to read naturally just by exposure to print results in misguided instructional

3 Curtis, S. (1977) *Genie: A linguistic study of a modern-day "wild child."* New York: Academic Press. Also, the Francois Truffaut film, The Wild Child, depicts the case of Victor, an abandoned child discovered in the woods and brought to an asylum in France in 1798. The film was written about in Roger Shattuck's *The forbidden experiment: The story of the wild boy of Aveyron*. New York: Washington Square Press, 1980.

practices. Although we have recently passed through an era of "whole language," vestiges of these beliefs continue to be visible in publications and popular programs. Because of the extensive research base now available on which to base a consensus, education in many respects is beginning to assimilate more current information about the prevalence, causes, and remedies for reading difficulty.

Spoken and Written Language Differ

Listen to these passages read aloud; what is special about the language in each of these texts? Is it like the language we speak?

Narrative Text:

> . . . Stuart peered ahead into the gathering storm, but saw nothing except gray waves with white crests. The world seemed cold and ominous. Stuart glanced behind him. There came the sloop, boiling along fast, rolling up a bow wave and gaining steadily.
>
> "Look out, Stuart! Look out where you're going!"
>
> Stuart strained his eyes and suddenly, dead ahead, right in the path of the Wasp, he saw an enormous paper bag looming up on the surface of the pond. The bag was empty and riding high, its open end gaping wide like the mouth of a cave . . . —*Stuart Little*[4]

Expository Text:

> . . . Among canine predators, puppies get an early start. Adult wolves will playfully ambush youngsters, and then allow them to tag along on hunts at three months of age. Occasionally an adult will step on a pup and hold it down, a playful gesture which biologists feel may duplicate that used by adult males and females to affirm rank within the pack. —*The World of Baby Animals*[5]

4 White, 1973.
5 Hodgson, 1995.

When we read, we usually read a special form of "standard English" that differs from spoken, conversational language in many ways. It is more formal and tightly constructed. Meaning is conveyed through a set of arbitrary written symbols that must be accurately processed. Phrases are not punctuated with "uh-like-you know" or repetitions of words. Choice of vocabulary varies. Complete the comparison of spoken and written language in the following chart as well as you can.

LETRS

Written Language Differs From Oral

- Speech sounds
- Printed symbols
- Vocabulary
- Sentence structure
- Paragraphs
- Overall structure (discourse)
- Context in which language is used

Slide 8

Exercise #2: Comparison of Spoken and Written Language

Compare some of the characteristics of spoken language and written language; refer to the previous excerpts to note the special qualities of written language.

	Spoken	Written
Speech Sounds		
Vocabulary		

	Spoken	Written
Sentence Structure		
Paragraphs		
Overall Structure		
Available Context		

One reason why learning to read and write is challenging is that a reader encounters a different language from that of conversation—the language of books and of academic discourse. The literate person has learned a special language and can decipher the writing system in which it is coded.

"Why am I talking this loud? Because I'm wrong."

What's Special About an Alphabet?

Types of Writing Systems

- Logographic: uses symbols to directly represent concepts (Chinese radicals)
- Syllabic: uses symbols for vowel-consonant or consonant-vowel combinations (Cherokee)
- Alphabetic: uses letters for single speech sounds, has consonant and vowel letters (English, Russian, Greek)

Slide 9

Writing systems evolved slowly over many thousands of years, but alphabetic writing is a recent achievement in human evolution. The first writing systems were pictograms that directly represented, or made a picture of, the meaning. More abstract symbolic systems evolved, but they used symbols to represent meaningful units (logographs). Mayan glyphs and ancient Chinese radicals were examples of logographic writing systems that did not rely on an alphabet. Many early and existing writing systems represented whole words, meaningful parts of words (morphemes), or syllables rather than individual speech sounds. About nine-tenths of the world's 4,000 to 6,000 existing spoken languages have no indigenous written form, let alone an alphabet.

Pictograms that directly represent meaning (hieroglyphics):

Logographs that abstractly represent meaning, not sound (Chinese radicals):

Syllabic symbols that directly represent whole syllables (Cherokee):

sa se si so su sʌ

Alphabetic symbols that represent consonants and vowels, or individual phonemes (Greek, Russian):

α β χ δ ε φ γ η ι φ κ λ

б в г д е ж з и к л м н

Exercise #3: Reflections on Writing Systems

Look at the previous samples of writing systems. Reflect and share:

- Have you ever learned a writing system other than the English alphabet?
- If so, was the system an alphabetic system?
- Do you remember what it was like to learn that system?

Awareness of Speech Sounds and the Alphabetic Principle

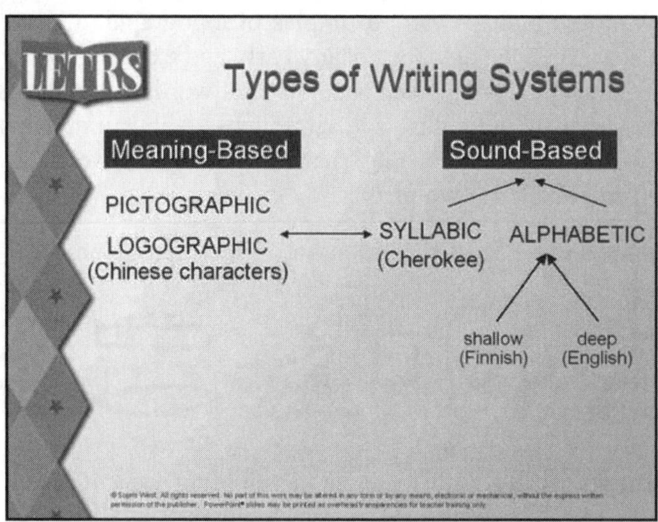

Slide 10

We can classify writing systems according to the level of language they represent. Sound-based systems can represent whole syllables or individual speech sounds. In addition, alphabetic systems can be "shallow" or "deep." (Please note, these are linguistic terms, not value judgments!) In a "shallow" or "transparent" alphabetic orthography such as Finnish or Spanish, the sound-symbol correspondences in the alphabetic writing system are regular and predictable, with one sound represented by one symbol or letter. Those letters represent the individual speech sounds in a system. Once we learn the sound that goes with a letter, we can read the words by using that code.

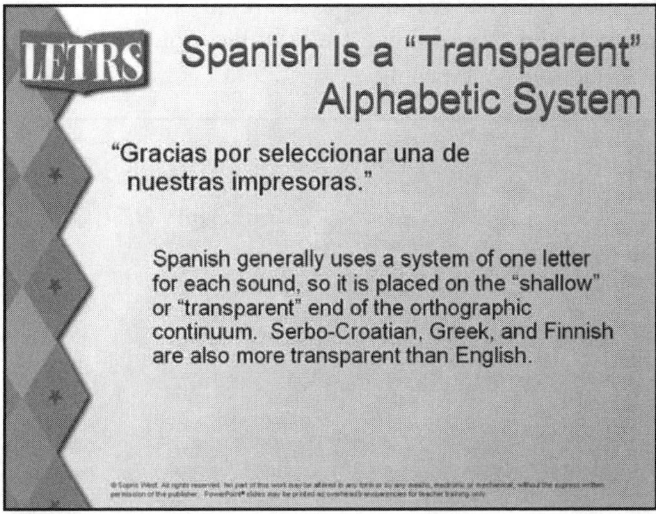

Slide 11

In Spanish, the spoken syllable units and sound sequences are more stable than those of English. Therefore, the letters that represent syllable patterns in Spanish writing are easy to associate with consonant-vowel combinations, such as *mi*, *me*, *ma*, *mo*, and *mu*. Yet, Spanish writing is not a syllabic writing system, even though the sounds in whole syllables are often taught together. Spanish uses an alphabetic orthography that represents the sound or phonemic level of spoken language. The Cherokee language, on the other hand, is a true syllabary with one symbol representing one whole syllable.

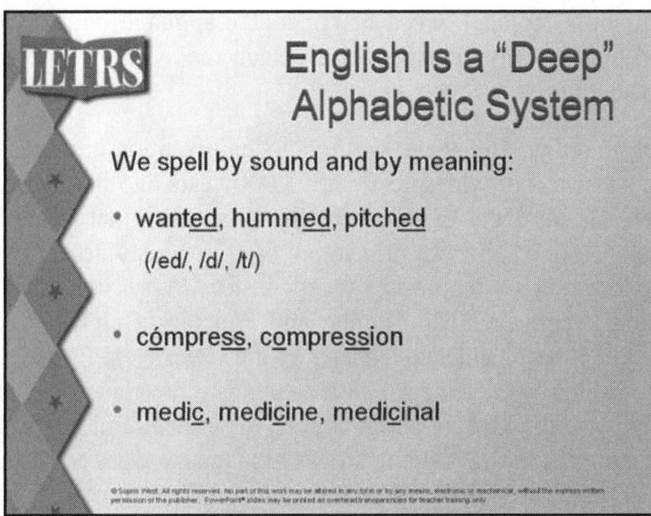

Slide 12

English, in contrast, is a "deep" or "opaque" alphabetic orthography. Its spelling system represents morphemes (meaningful parts) as well as speech sounds. For example, in *compression*, the *com* is unaccented and the vowel is indistinct (schwa). The final *ss* in the *press* root of *compression* sounds like /sh/. In the noun *compress*, the vowel in *com* is accented and sounds like "short o." The final *ss* in press sounds like /s/. The spelling of each word, however, shows the prefix *com* and the root *press*

as meaningful units. The spelling does not represent the variability in our pronunciation of the sounds in the prefix or the root. Thus, we spell these words by sound *and* by meaning.

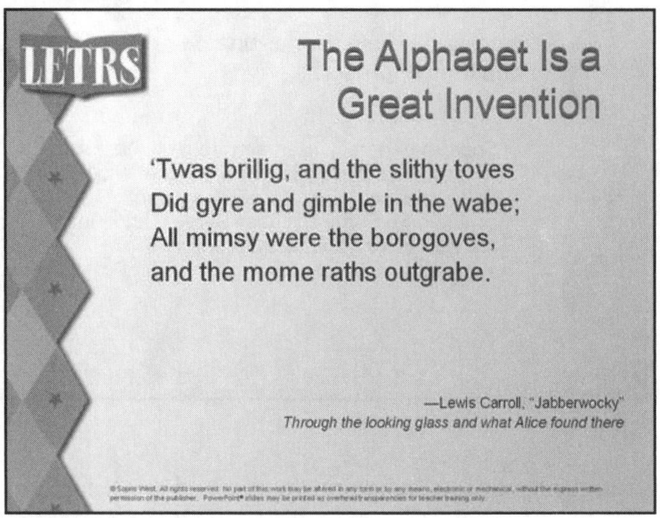

Slide 13

Alphabetic writing systems developed when humans discovered that speech sounds, or phonemes, could be represented individually. Such a system, its inventors must have realized, was efficient and liberating. Only a limited set of symbols was needed to represent any word and those could be combined infinitely to represent an entire language. No longer would literacy require memorization of hundreds or even thousands of unique symbols for each word or concept. Language could be written down and read by anyone who could match the symbols to the sounds they represented.

In spite of its utility, alphabetic writing eluded invention until about 5,000 years ago and was not widespread until 3,000 years ago in Greek civilization. Why? Because the existence of the phoneme—that which a letter represents—is not a self-evident, natural, or consciously accessible understanding for humans. People are "wired" instead to process speech for the meaning it conveys. The Semitic and Phoenician alphabet, invented around 3500 B.C. and adapted later by the Greeks and Romans, was an astonishing achievement of meta-linguistic awareness—that is, the ability to think about and reflect on the structure of language itself. If insight into the building blocks of language were easily achieved, then alphabets would have been invented much more readily and used much more widely.

" 'Twas brillig, and the slithy toves Did gyre and gimble in the wabe; All mimsy were the borogoves, and the mome raths outgrabe fifty basis points."

Of all the languages in the world, the alphabetic writing system of English is comparatively difficult. Languages such as Spanish, Italian, Serbo-Croatian, and Finnish are more phonetic. They are closer to having one letter for each sound.

"Congratulazioni per l'acuisto della stampante" can be read with relatively little difficulty if the vowel sounds are known to the reader.

Do you remember how you learned to read? The following exercise will help you to relive that experience and to reflect on it with your colleagues.

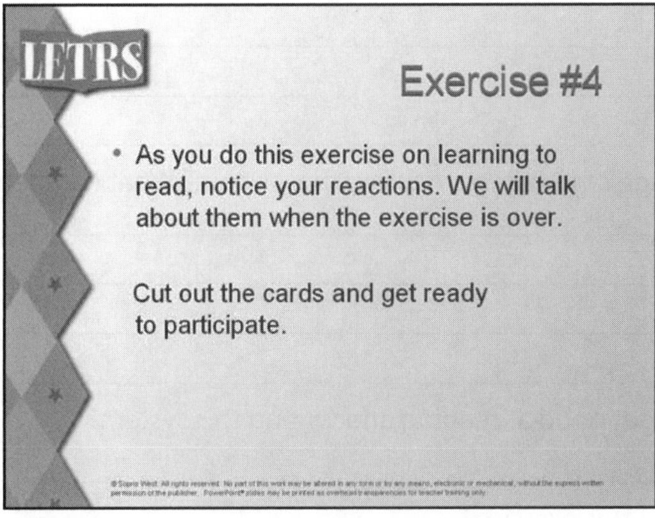

Slide 14

Exercise #4: Simulation of Learning to Read

After we complete this exercise, we will talk about it. Be prepared to share your reflections on these questions: What was challenging for you? What did you do to adapt to the challenge of learning a new symbol system? How much practice would you need to get good at reading and writing this system? What were you feeling as you carried out this exercise?

1. Prepare! Cut out the symbol and sight word cards on pages 63 and 65 of this module. You will learn the sound-symbol correspondences for ten consonants and three vowels and will apply that knowledge to reading and writing words.
2. Follow your instructor as you are guided through the following steps:
   a. Imitating the correct production of phonemes, describing how they are articulated, and matching phonemes with symbols.
   b. Blending sounds into words.
   c. Spelling words with sound-symbol cards.
   d. Writing symbols for sounds that are dictated.
   e. Making a word chain: Start with one word and change it sound by sound when the teacher says a new word. Use your symbol cards to show the changes and make the new word.
   f. Memorizing some "sight" words so that sentence reading is possible.
   g. Reading phrases and sentences.
   h. Writing phrases and sentences.

Response:

What was challenging for you? ______________________________

What did you do to adapt to the challenge of learning a new symbol system? What compensatory skills did you try to employ? ______________________________

How much practice would you need to get good at reading and writing this system? ______________

What were you feeling as you carried out this exercise? ______________________________

What the Mind Does When It Reads

Slide 15

The mechanics of fluent, accurate reading are quite remarkable. When engrossed in what he or she is reading, a proficient reader scans the print effortlessly, extracting meaning and sifting through it, making connections between new ideas in the text and existing knowledge, and interpreting according to his or her purposes. The reader figures out new words and names very quickly and with minimal effort, consciously employing a sounding out strategy only when necessary. He or she reads without being distracted by problems with word recognition. If the reader happens to misread a word or phrase or does not comprehend a word or phrase, he or she quickly adapts by rereading to clarify what was unclear. While reading, the reader forms a mental model or schema for the meanings just extracted. That schema or mental construction has a logical framework into which he or she files the information to remember.

The attainment of reading skill has fascinated psychologists and invited more study than any other aspect of learning. The study of proficient reading and reading problems has earned more funding increases over the last few years than any other public health issue studied by the National Institute of Child Health and Human Development. Because of programmatic research efforts over many years, scientific consensus on some important issues in reading development and reading instruction has been reached.

One important understanding is that the behavior of fluent reading for comprehension depends largely on the ability to know what the words say. Reading is the product of two major sets of subskills—decoding and comprehension. Printed words cannot be interpreted unless they are accurately pronounced or named (*abroad* is not *aboard*; *scarred* is not *scared*; *etymology* is not *entymology*). A fluent reader, however, carries out the process of word naming with deceptive ease. Word recognition (word naming) occurs below the level of conscious analysis so rapidly and effortlessly that the fluent reader is not aware of it. Word recognition in a good reader, in fact, is served by the middle (temporal-parietal-occipital junction) and back (occipital) areas of the left hemisphere in the networks specialized for automatic association of print symbols with speech. In this way, the frontal areas so important in abstract and higher level reasoning are freed up in the service of comprehension.

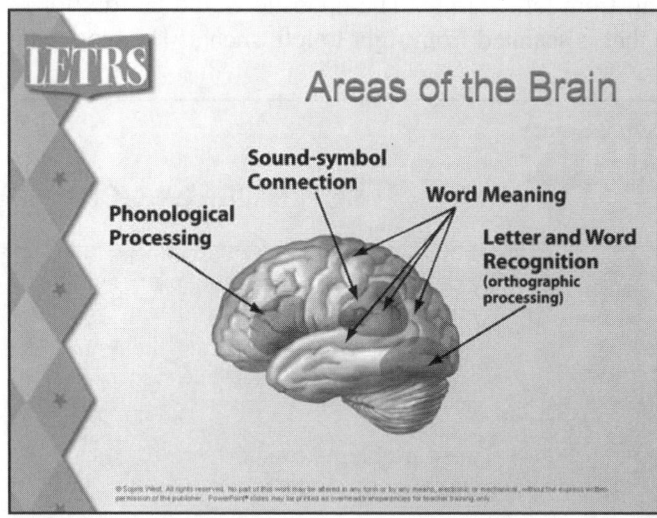

Slide 16

Eye Movements and Reading

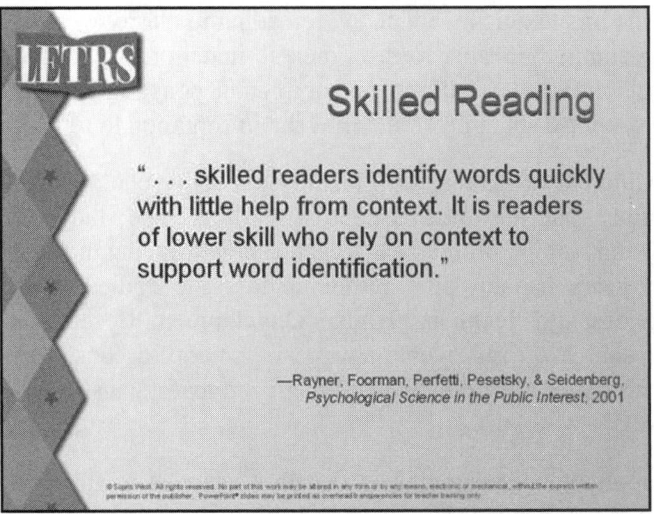

Slide 17

Watch the eyes of a person scanning text at a normal rate. The eye seems to be ahead of the voice when we read aloud—and indeed, it is. The precision eye-movement research of scientists such as Keith Rayner and Andrew Pollatsek at the Massachusetts Institute of Technology have shown in many experiments over twenty-five years that the reading eye fixates on most content words (especially nouns and verbs) in a rapid series of stops and jumps called fixations and saccades. When fixated, the eye rests for about .25 seconds (250 milliseconds) on a content word and takes in a span of about seven to nine letters to the right of the fixation and three to four letters to the left before it jumps over to the next fixation point. More letters are processed to the right of the fixation if the eye is scanning from left to right. The opposite would be true for reading a language that is scanned from right to left, such as Hebrew.

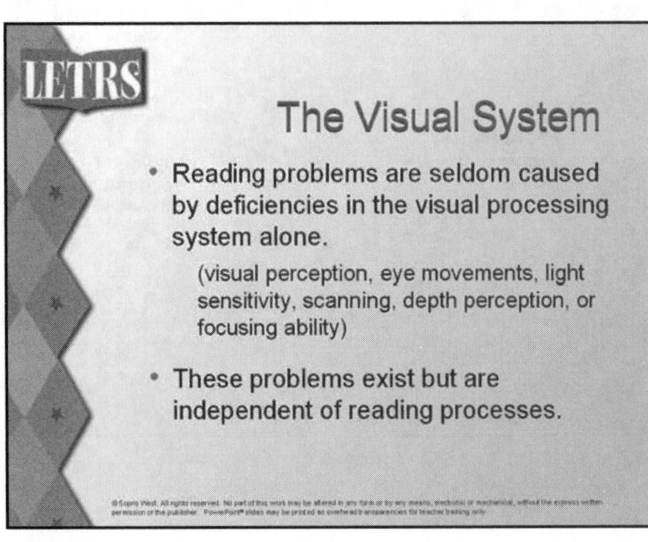

Slide 18

Although we may not be aware of it, we do not skip over words, read print selectively, or recognize words by sampling a few letters of the print, as theorists such as Frank Smith proposed in the 1970s. Reading is accomplished with letter-wise processing of the word. Fluent readers take in each and every letter of print. Thus we can distinguish *severe* from *several*, *antidote* from *anecdote*; and *primeval* from *prime evil*. Better readers can see the internal details of printed words and match them to the individual speech sounds that make up the spoken word.[6] Even when "chunks" are processed, they can be analyzed into their individual phoneme-grapheme correspondences on demand.[7]

When poor readers seem to have trouble tracking print smoothly from left to right, their jerky eye movements and regressions (looking back) are a *consequence* of poor reading, not a *cause*. Only a very few reading problems are actually caused by visual scanning and tracking deficits. Children who have eye-focusing or eye-coordination problems are readily diagnosed and treated by ophthalmologists and optometrists—but rarely is a reading problem cured by treatment of the eyes.

Four Processing Systems

The following diagram is helpful for understanding the functional systems involved in reading. These systems are discussed at length in Marilyn Adams's landmark book, *Beginning to Read: Thinking and Learning About Print*[8] and two recent summary articles in *Scientific American* and *Psychological Science in the Public Interest*[9]. The schematic representation of the systems is an oversimplification, of course, as many neurological networks support proficient reading.

That reading depends on the coordinated use of multiple brain systems suggests a well-documented inference: reading problems may originate in any or all of the processing systems. Subtypes of poor readers may have specific problems in one of these processing systems. If reading instruction is well designed, it will educate all of the functions: recognition and fast processing of sounds, letter patterns, morphemes, word meanings, phrases, sentences, and longer passages.

6 See Rayner and Pollatschek (1989) for more complete descriptions of eye movement studies in reading.

7 The work of Linnea Ehri has unraveled the mechanisms of word recognition. See Gaskins et al., 1996, and Ehri, 1997.

8 Adams, 1990.

9 Rayner et al., 2001, 2002.

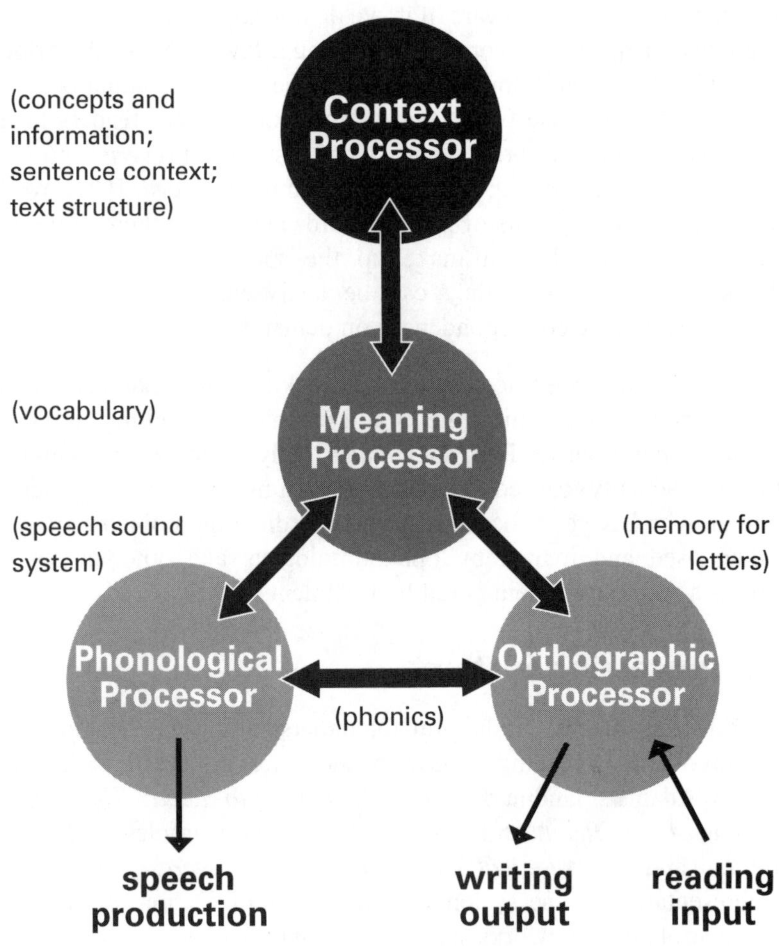
(concepts and information; sentence context; text structure)
Context Processor
(vocabulary)
Meaning Processor
(speech sound system)
(memory for letters)
Phonological Processor
Orthographic Processor
(phonics)
speech production
writing output
reading input

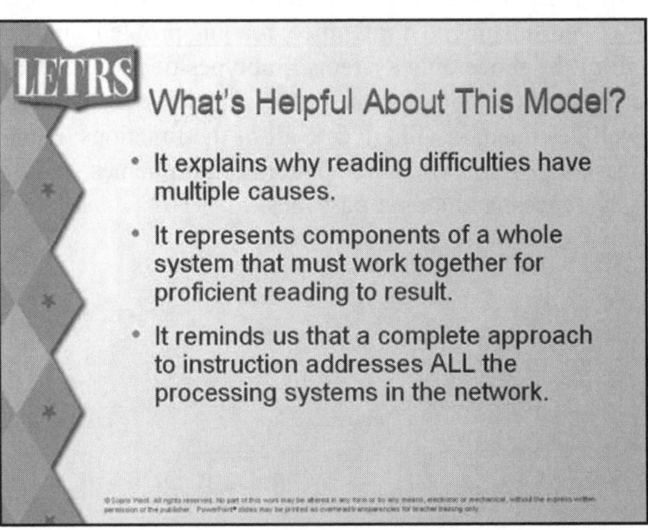
LETRS
What's Helpful About This Model?
It explains why reading difficulties have multiple causes.
It represents components of a whole system that must work together for proficient reading to result.
It reminds us that a complete approach to instruction addresses ALL the processing systems in the network.

Slide 19

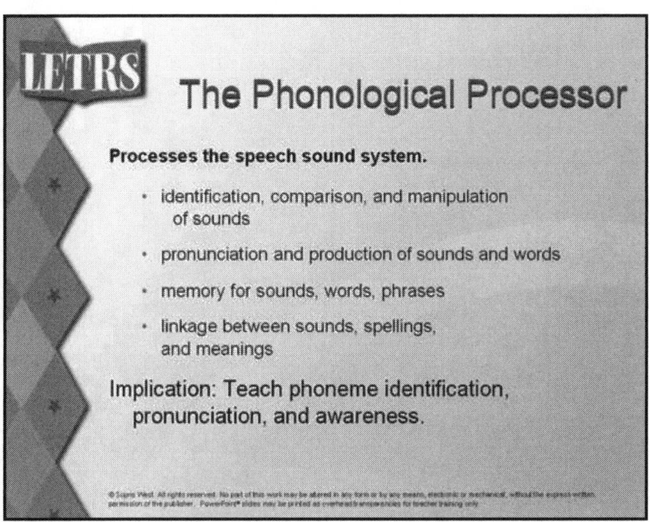

Slide 20

The Phonological Processor. This network enables us to perceive, remember, interpret, and produce the speech sound system of our own language and learn the sounds of other languages. The phonological processor allows us to imitate and produce stress patterns, including the rise and fall of the voice during phrasing. It is responsible for such functions as:

- Establishing identities for the phoneme or distinguishing speech sounds in a language;
- Remembering the words in a phrase or the sounds in a word;
- Comparing words that sound similar, such as *reintegrate* and *reiterate*;
- Retrieving specific words from the mental dictionary (lexicon) and producing the speech sounds;
- Holding the sounds of a word in memory so that a word can be written down; and
- Taking apart the sounds in a word so that they can be matched with alphabetic symbols.

The phonological processor detects, stores, and retrieves the phonemes and sound sequences in spoken language; the orthographic processor detects, stores, and retrieves the graphemes and letter sequences in print.

The Orthographic Processor

Processes letters, letter patterns, and whole words.

- recognition and formation of letters
- association of letters with speech sounds
- recognition of letter sequences and patterns
- fluent recognition of whole words
- recall of letters for spelling

Implication: Call attention to the internal details and patterns of printed words. Strive for automatic ("by sight") word recognition as phonics is learned.

Slide 21

The orthographic processor. The orthographic processing system visually perceives and recognizes letters, punctuation marks, spaces, and words. We rely on the orthographic processor when we copy lines of print, recognize words as whole units, or remember letter sequences for spelling. When we look at print, its features are filtered, identified, and matched to images of letters or letter sequences already in memory. If the letters or letter sequences are familiar, we associate them with sounds and meanings. We have no trouble interpreting widely varying print forms, including individual handwriting styles, type fonts, or uppercase and lowercase letters. The size, style, and case of print are not major factors in word recognition once a reader knows letters and letter-sound relationships.

The orthographic processing system stores information about print necessary for word recognition and for spelling. The speed with which letters are recognized and recalled is very important for proficient reading. Obviously, print images must be associated with meaning for reading comprehension to occur.

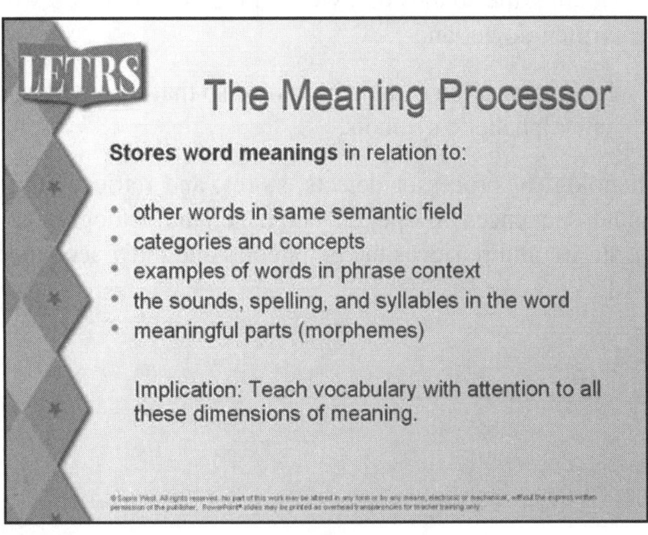

Slide 22

The Meaning Processor. According to the four-part processing model, recognizing words as meaningful entities requires communication between the phonological processor, orthographic processor, and meaning processor. The meaningless association of speech sounds with print may allow us to "read" a foreign language without knowing what it means, to read nonsense words, or to read a new name by sounding it out, but unless the meaning processor is accessed no comprehension is possible. The meaning processor stores the inventory of known words and also constructs the meanings of any new words that are named during reading. The context of the passage supports the construction of those meanings.

A word filed in the mental dictionary is multidimensional; its image has sound, spelling, morphological structure, and a syntactic role. The meaning processor is structured according to a number of semantic organization features, such as synonym relationships, roots and other morphemes, spelling patterns, common meaning associations, and connotations. It expands and reorganizes itself as new vocabulary is learned.

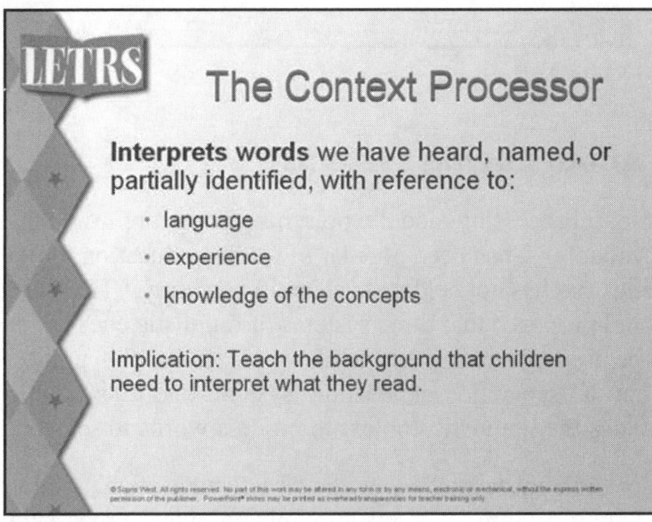

Slide 23

The Context Processor. The context processor influences the meaning processor in many ways. The context in which a word occurs is the sentence and sentence sequence in which it is embedded. The context provides the referent for a word's meaning. For example, many words have multiple meanings but only one is used within a specific sentence. The spelling of a word such as *passed* or *past* is determined by its meaning in the context of a sentence:

- Fiedler *passed* the ball to the wide receiver for the touchdown.

Context helps us rapidly find a meaning in our mental dictionary once a word has been named:

- That idea provided a *segue* between the introduction and the body of the speech.

Context has only a very limited role in facilitating word naming itself. Word recognition and pronunciation are primarily the job of the phonological and orthographic processors.

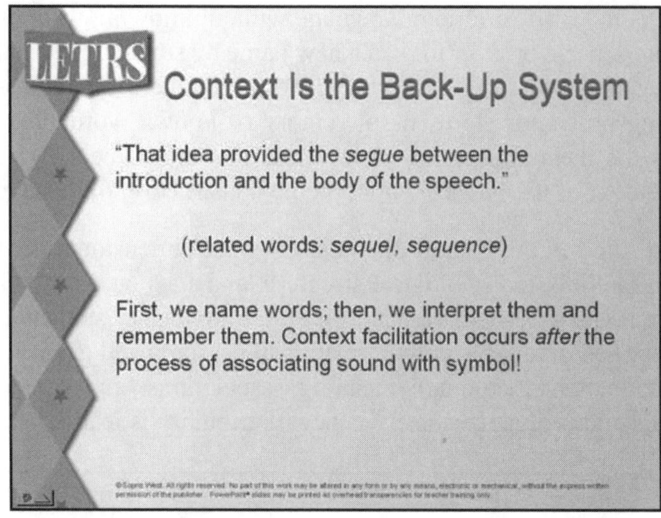

Slide 24

What About Cueing Systems?

Our four-part processing model represents a departure from the "3 cueing system" model that has been popular in reading education for the last two decades but that has not held up to scientific scrutiny.[10] The "3 cueing system" model proposed that three systems of linguistic cues reside in a text and can be used by a reader to decode words: a "graphophonic" or "visual" system; a "semantic" or meaning system; and a "syntactic" system that provides the linguistic context to process words in sentences.

The major problem with the way the "3 cueing system" model has been used is that it minimizes the role of phonological processing in word recognition and treats the phonological and orthographic systems as if they were one and the same. Further, it overemphasizes the role of context and meaning in word recognition, and leads teachers astray when it encourages them to say to a student, "What would make sense here?" instead of asking a student to apply phonic decoding skills before resorting to context. Guessing at words on the basis of context, even with reference to an initial consonant sound, is not a good habit to encourage when children are first learning to read. Later reading fluency depends on early mastery of associations between letters, letter patterns, and speech sounds. Moreover, context use is an accurate way to identify unknown words only about one out of four to one out of ten times!

10 For a complete review of the origin and use of this model, see Adams, 1998.

Exercise #5: Which Processors Are Involved?

Read this passage about a sports event:

> *Although he has had mediocre results all season, Moseley pulled off a victory today in the World Moguls competition. Consequently, he secured a spot on the U.S. Olympic Moguls Ski Team. He could not have done better.*

Now, select which processing system or systems [phonological processor (PP), orthographic processor (OP), meaning processor (MP), or context processor (CP)] might support each of the following activities associated with reading. Most tasks draw on more than one processing system:

1. Recognizing that the right meaning of *spot* is "a place on the team roster." PP OP MP CP
2. Noticing that the word "world" uses an unusual spelling for the /er/ sound. PP OP MP CP
3. Sounding out *mediocre* and coming up with "med-i-o-cray." PP OP MP CP
4. Sounding out *mediocre*, mispronouncing it, and correcting the pronunciation after the meaning of the word is recognized. PP OP MP CP

5. After reading the phrase *pulled off*, recognizing that it is a figure of speech and it means "accomplished in spite of the odds." PP OP MP CP
6. Looking at the word *mogul* and noticing that the spelling could be "mogle" just by syllable spelling rules. PP OP MP CP

7. Noticing that every word that ends in a /v/ sound spells it with *ve*. PP OP MP CP

8. Aurally remembering the lines of this story after hearing them read aloud several times. PP OP MP CP

9. Knowing that *consequently* means "as a consequence of." PP OP MP CP

10. Reading and writing words such as *all* and *off* as whole words, without thinking consciously about the individual letter-sound relationships in them. PP OP MP CP

11. Isolating and pronouncing the vowel sound in the word *ski*. PP OP MP CP
12. Figuring out that *moguls* must be a type of skiing, based on the phrase in which it is used. PP OP MP CP

How Children Learn to Read

The Continuum of Reading Development

Models of proficient reading and an understanding of the many cognitive systems that support it do not tell us how people learn to read. The proficient reader amalgamates information from all four major processing systems rapidly, accurately, and often effortlessly. However, the role that each processor plays in reading and the functional relationships among the processing systems change as reading skill develops.

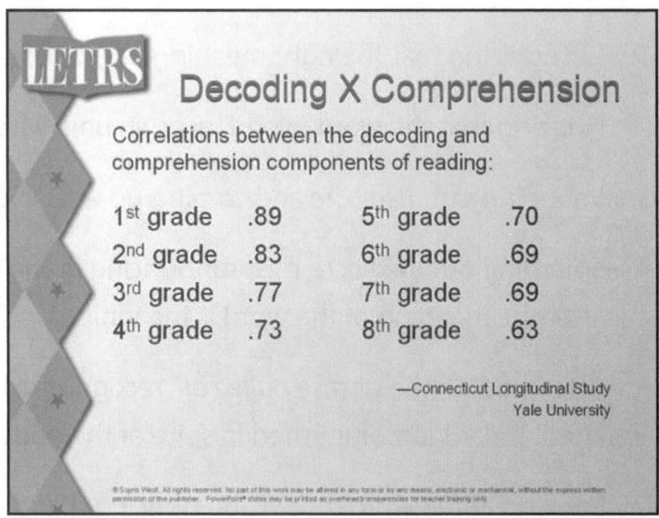

Slide 25

In the Connecticut Longitudinal Study, conducted at Yale University for over 20 years, a group of 400 kindergarten children were followed through their schooling.[11] Testing the children every year with the Woodcock-Johnson Achievement Test, researchers were able to see how the relationship between decoding abilities (real word reading and phonic analysis of nonsense words) and passage comprehension changed with each grade. Initially, the ability to decode—the ability to read the words accurately—accounted for about 80% of passage reading comprehension ability. (The proportion of variance accounted for in one variable by another variable is obtained by squaring a correlation between the two.) Phonic decoding and fast word recognition was the primary task for first grade children to master. By fourth grade, about 50% of the ability to comprehend passages was accounted for by the ability to read the words and apply phonics to new words. As students learned to recognize words, other components of reading—such as knowledge of vocabulary, higher level reasoning skills, and reading fluency—became more important to reading success.

11 Foorman, et al., 1997. The Connecticut Longitudinal Study has been conducted at Yale University under the direction of Sally Shaywitz, M.D. The Foorman chapter is based on the study results.

A Description of Reading "Stages"

LETRS

Chall's Stages of Reading Development (1983)

- Prereading; pre-alphabetic (0)
- Initial reading or alphabetic decoding (1)
  - Early phonetic
  - Later phonetic
- Confirmation and fluency (2)
- Reading to learn (3)

Slide 26

Jeanne Chall, Harvard's well-known professor of reading, developed the first stage theory of reading development in 1983. Dr. Chall argued that *reading* was a word with very different meanings for children and adults of different age and skill levels. In brief, her conceptual outline of reading stages differentiated the characteristics and demands of reading in six major periods of reading development. Her stages described well what children typically had to master as they progressed through a school curriculum. Chall's stage framework is still useful in understanding how the challenges of learning and teaching reading change over time. Her stages were defined as follows:

0 Prereading; also called pre-alphabetic, logographic, and preconventional (typical of preschool through late kindergarten)

1 Initial Reading or Alphabetic Decoding; also called alphabetic decoding stage for learning to read words (typical of late kindergarten through early grade two)

2 Confirmation and Fluency (typical of grades two and three)

3 Reading to Learn (typical of grades four to eight)

4 Multiple Points of View (typical of high school)

5 Construction and Reconstruction (typical of college and adulthood)

Subsequent reading research has modified Chall's framework, especially in the areas of early word recognition and spelling. Current theories of early word reading development emphasize the simultaneous and reciprocal growth of skill in all major processing systems (Ehri, 1996; Rayner et al., 2001; Share & Stanovich, 1995) and the "amalgamation" of sound, spelling, and meaning in word learning. Phonological processing, orthographic processing, and meaning-making develop on a continuum, in tandem. Fluency is an essential component of skill development at each

stage of learning. Verbal comprehension and vocabulary develop from the time children enter school. Exposure to text and reading practice are critical in moving the growth process along.

Ehri's phases of word reading development, summarized in the chart below, are widely referenced because their description rests on multiple experiments conducted over many years that have been replicated by other researchers. In Ehri's model, the ability to recognize many words "by sight" during fluent reading rests on the ability to map phonemes to graphemes, or to master the alphabetic principle. At first, children may recognize a few words as wholes, by their configuration or the context in which they are found, such as labels on boxes or lists. However, progress in reading an alphabetic system occurs only if children learn how letters and sounds are connected. It is impossible for children to memorize more than a few dozen words without insight into the purpose of alphabetic symbols. Alphabetic learning is acquired through progressive differentiation of both the sounds in words and the letter sequences in print. Phoneme awareness is the foundation upon which letter-sound association can be constructed.

As students learn phoneme-grapheme mapping, their orthographic processors begin to store memories for recurring letter patterns in the form of "chunks"—syllable spellings, common endings and word parts, and high frequency words. Accurate and fluent perception of chunks, however, rests on phoneme-grapheme mapping.

Phases of Word Reading Development (After Ehri, 1996)

Phase →⇒	Logographic	Novice Alphabetic	Mature Alphabetic	Orthographic
How Child Reads Familiar Words	Rote learning of incidental visual features of a word; no letter-sound awareness	Partial use of letter-sound correspondence; initial sound and salient consonants	Pronunciation of whole word on basis of complete phoneme-grapheme mapping	Variously by phonemes, syllabic units, morpheme units, and whole words
How Child Reads Unfamiliar Words	Guessing constrained by context or memory of text	Constrained by context; gets first sound and guesses	Full use of phoneme-grapheme correspondence; blends all sounds left to right; begins to use analogy to known patterns	Sequential and hierarchical decoding;notices familiar parts first, reads by analogy to similar known words
Other Indicators	Dependent on context; few words; errors and confusions; cannot read text	Similar-appearing words are confused	Rapid, unitized reading of whole familiar words is increasing	Remembers multisyllabic words; analogizes easily, associates word structure with meaning
Spelling	Strings letters together, assigns meaning without representing sounds in words	Represents a few salient sounds, such as beginning and ending consonants; fills in other letters randomly; some letter names for sounds	Phonetically accurate; beginning to incorporate conventional letter sequences and patterns; sight word knowledge increasing	Word knowledge includes language of origin, morphemes, syntactic role, ending rules, prefix, suffix & root forms

Slide 27

The "phases" involve gradual integration of information from the four processing systems that underlie word recognition. To illustrate, children at the beginning decoding stage, who have been exposed often to the print in books, often show surprising awareness of the letter sequences and orthographic patterns that characterize English spelling. They may not associate familiar letters and letter sequences with speech sounds, but they know something about the sequences of letters in print just from looking at so many examples. For example, they may know that *-ck* is used at the ends of words, not the beginnings; that letters can be doubled at the ends of words but not at the beginnings; that only certain letters are doubled; and that syllables typically contain a vowel letter. Orthographic knowledge, knowledge of the spelling system itself, develops when the student has internalized awareness of the sounds to which the letters in words correspond.

Case Study Examples of Early Reading and Spelling Development

Student A: Logographic Reader and Speller*

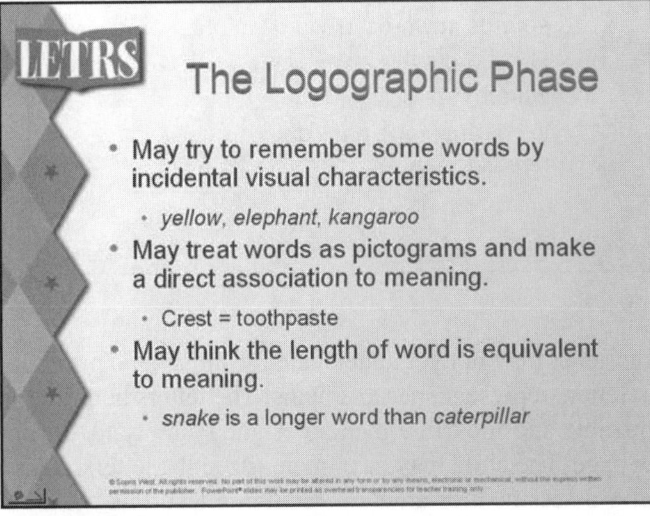

Slide 28

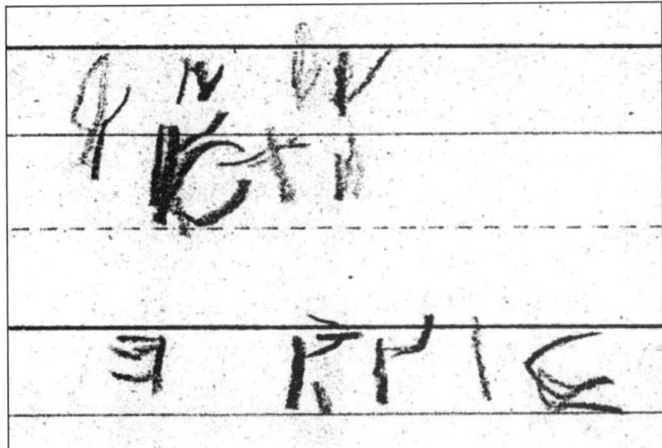

Student A: Writing sample, September.

*Kindergarten writing examples provided by Pat Tyborowski, classroom teacher and coauthor of *Focus on /F/onemes*, a kindergarten instructional program.

LETRS

Student Writing Sample A

Beginning kindergartener, September:

- What letters are recognizable?
- Is there left to right representation of the sounds in words or words in phrases?
- How would this child "read" back what was written?
- What are some basic things this child needs to learn?

Slide 29

This kindergartener may not yet understand the alphabetic principle—the concept that letters represent speech sounds. The letters he writes are not fully recognizable and look like marks designed simply to fill up some space on the page. The child may have memorized the letters in his name. On a DIBELS assessment or an early screening test, this child may not know what is being asked if the teacher says, "What is the first *sound* in this word—dog?" The child might say, "Bow-wow!"

This child may not yet understand that individual speech sounds are the building blocks of spoken words. Nevertheless, he may begin to observe the visual characteristics of print, such as left to right progression, the spacing of words, the alternating patterns of letters, the use of capitals at the beginnings of words, or the fact that certain combinations exist. We do not know how many letter names this child may have learned; he may know some even though he does not understand how the letters represent the sounds.

Student B: Novice Alphabetic Phase

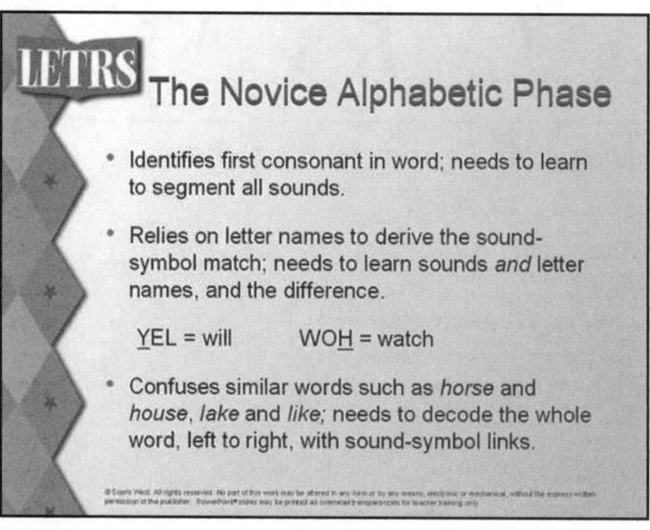

Slide 30

	Student spelling	Word
1.	red	red
2.	mks	name
3.	beD	bed
4.	had	lady
5.	fer	fish
6.	Net	men
7.	Bittl	boat
8.	gaitl	girl
9.	KerlD	color
10.	Arihkl	angry
11.	tku	thankyou
12.	Pcragl	people
13.	GOD	dog
14.	BaKlg	boy

Student B: Invented spellings, beginning grade 1.

LETRS

Student Writing Sample B

- Where in the word are the speech sounds this child represents quite consistently?
- Are there any letter names used for sounds?
- Are there any words with “random” letters put in as fillers?
- Any examples indicating that left to right sequence is not fully established?

Slide 31

In this phase, the child's primary task is learning the sound-symbol correspondences that will be necessary for decoding new words. Success in decoding depends on the development of phoneme awareness as well as the ability to remember and differentiate the letters used to spell individual speech sounds. Phonological and orthographic awareness is necessary for accurate and efficient word recognition. Children who do acquire speed with the elements—recognition of letters, sound-symbol links, syllables, and meaningful parts—are most likely to be proficient readers at the end of third grade when high-stakes testing typically begins.

This child may confuse printed words that share letters and that are not distinctive enough to be recognized by their overall configuration. For example, *house*, *horse*, and *how* are visually similar and unless the child can process all the letters and sounds, the words are likely to be mistaken for one another. On DIBELS testing or early screening measures, this child is likely to do well at identifying the initial sound in words but may be weak at blending all the sounds in an unknown word.

The novice alphabetic learner is ready to learn how each sound is typically spelled and how to blend letter-sound correspondences into simple words. For a few weeks, months, or even longer, a novice alphabetic reader might expend a good deal of attention and mental effort to break words apart, blend the sounds, and approach new words sound-by-sound as symbols are linked. As individual phoneme-grapheme associations are learned and used, they become rapid and automatic and the new reader "chunks" them into patterns. After sufficient exposure and practice, whole words are recognized as units. This kind of "sight" word recognition, however, depends on the reader being able to process rapidly the internal details of the word letter by letter so as to store a complete image of the word in memory.

Student A, May Writing: Mature Alphabetic Phase

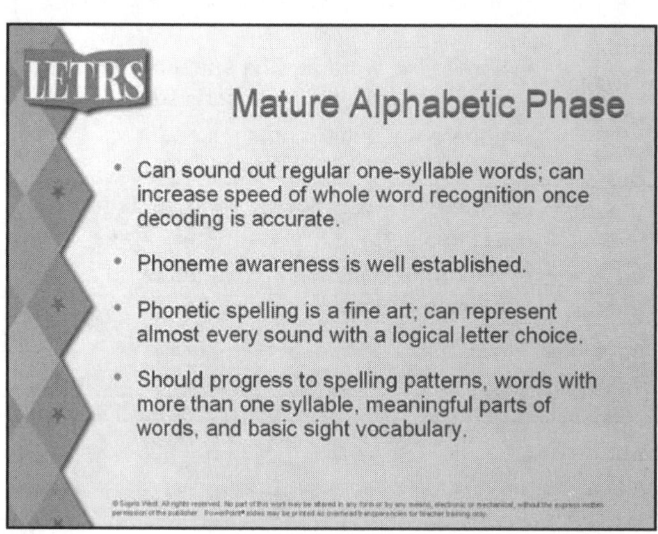

Slide 32

My trip
Woshintin Dc it is
65 dgree I m going
To play at woshintin Dc
Im going to pack chlos
I going to see the wit
hous I wil see
presind bnt booshe

Student A: Writing sample, May.*

Student A, May Writing Sample

- Does this student represent most of the speech sounds in words?
- Are there examples of phonetically accurate spellings that are orthographically naïve?
- Explain the spelling of "clothes."
- Explain the spelling of "Bush."
- What else has this child learned since the beginning of the year?

Slide 33

Children who have a good handle on the most regular sound-symbol elements will generalize and teach themselves about others from exposure to examples. These are the "self-teachers" who pick up speed and insight about words as they store more and more examples of sound-spellings in memory. Children who are less able to compare words and figure out sound-symbol links will need continuing instruction in the entire sound-symbol correspondence system, especially for spelling.

Children at the mature alphabetic stage become good at generating a fairly complete and reasonable phonetic spelling. Simultaneously, they notice and store information about letter sequences in high frequency words and syllable patterns. The goal of this stage is to build fast and accurate word recognition and spelling so that words will not have to be laboriously sounded out. Fluency with the elements will build fluency with sentences and passages. The process of sounding out is a first step that builds the essential foundation for differentiating, remembering, and quickly recognizing words in print.

Many children do not complete the transition to orthographic reading and writing until the intermediate grades. Multisyllabic words must be conquered. There is more to decoding than basic phonics; developing readers also need to decompose words into syllables and morphemes, to develop recognition and spelling for unusual words (*yacht*, *colonel*, *Wednesday*), and to understand the structure of Latin-derived vocabulary.

Achieving Passage Reading Fluency With Comprehension

Slide 34

In second and third grade, with decoding skills learned well enough to support word recognition accuracy, children must consolidate their reading skills and build reading fluency. Their speed typically increases from about 60 words per minute correct at the end of first grade to about 120 words per minute in oral reading by the end of third grade. If this goal is not reached, reading will be too slow and inefficient to support comprehension. Speed and accuracy of oral passage reading in first through third grades predicts comprehension of passages on high-stakes examinations such as the Stanford 9 Achievement Test.

Extensive reading in material that can be read with accuracy is the best way for children to develop fluency. Better readers read more, and by reading more, get to be better readers. If children are too slow, a number of instructional techniques that involve repeated readings will help them come up to speed.

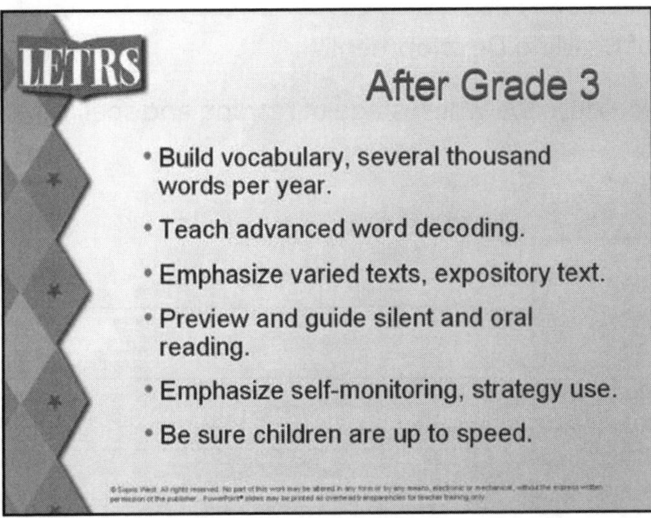

Slide 35

In the transition from third grade to fourth grade, the reading demands of the curriculum change. Fourth graders are expected to read independently, silently, and selectively, and teachers assume they have acquired the reading skills necessary to do so. Children must use text to gain information as well as to appreciate the joys of fiction, biography, history, and science. Reading instruction is usually targeted at those who are not at grade level, although many students need additional reading skill instruction. Among the skills that still need attention are the ability to regulate reading speed according to the purpose of an assignment, the ability to monitor one's comprehension, and the mental discipline of asking the author questions, stating or writing summaries of main ideas, and understanding the organization of a text.

Exercise #6: Describe the Child's Phase of Reading Development

Given examples of children's work, can you describe which stage of reading and spelling development each one might represent?*

Student C

LETRS

Exercise #6: Student C

In September, what phase of reading and spelling development did this child appear to be in?

What about the use of letters and numbers?

By May, what phase has this child achieved? Support your observations with references to specific words.

Slide 36

ABCDEFGHIJKL MNOPQRSTU
DADDY MOMMY
E AMM ANN A RIAAVM
AMNAMAAMAA AAAVVA
1 2 3 4 5 6 7 8 9 10 11 12 13 14 15 1
AAAA

Student C: Writing sample, September.

a wich toock the pretty pretty princess
and shee brot the princess and then the
wich toock the priness in to the cich
in and the wich tide the princess
to a char and then a prince savd
her and then thae livd haplee evr
aftr

Student C: Writing sample, April.

* **Note**: Examples provided by Pat Tyborowski, coauthor of *Focus on /F/onemes*, a kindergarten instructional program.

Student D, 6th Grade

LETRS

Exercise #6, Student D

This student is in 6th grade, but shows some of the characteristics of beginning readers and spellers.

- Are there developmental phase indicators in this student's writing?
- Would it be helpful to think about this child as being in a specific phase of reading and spelling development?

Slide 37

> "TITEL WAVE!" But befor she could do eny thing a dig hug hole opend up in the middel of the wave. The two gerles started to run, but the wave was tow fast for them. It suked them in the hole and then they startet floping around, they hit ther hedes on part of the rocy botom. They both got knoked out dead. When they woke up they were in a room whith a deap blue ceiing and the bed they were laing on was made of orol and the blanket was a dark blue tint over them. Gust then they herd the dore creek open. A girl with really long brown hair and a white sooba biving shurt and pants with a "sbc" on the shurt. Walked over to them and said "hellou" my name is Maddie, wats your name." I'm mary and shes ruby mary said. "Well come with me and lets get some food."

Student D: Writing sample, 6th Grade.

Components of Comprehensive Reading Instruction

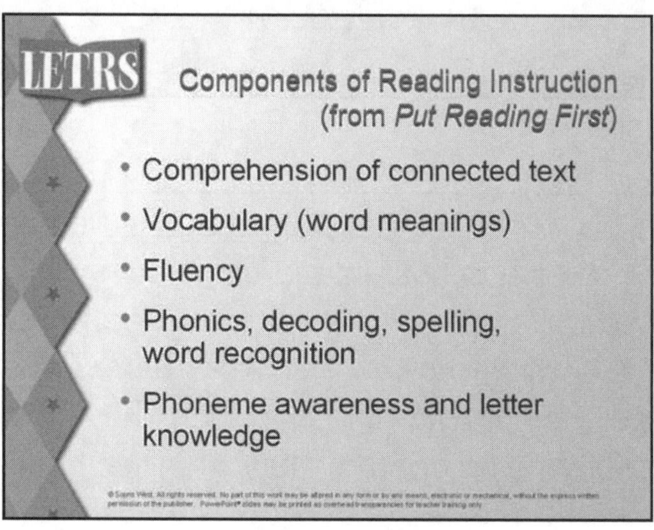

Slide 38

Agreement by experts in recent, comprehensive reviews of reading research is substantial: a successful teacher of reading enables children to comprehend and produce written language, generates enthusiasm and appreciation for reading and writing, and expertly teaches children how to decode, interpret, and spell new words from a foundation of linguistic awareness. Using valid and reliable assessments, the successful teacher adapts the pacing, content, and emphasis of instruction for individuals and groups. The teacher's choices are guided by knowledge of the critical skills and attitudes needed at each stage of reading development. Beginning reading skill is taught explicitly and systematically to children within an overall program of purposeful, engaging reading and writing.

Major Components of Research-Supported Reading Instruction

- Phonemic Awareness and Letter Knowledge
- Phonics, Decoding, Spelling, and Word Recognition
- Fluency
- Vocabulary (Knowledge of Word Meanings)
- Comprehension of Connected Text (Phrase, Sentence, Paragraph, Extended Discourse)
- Written Expression*
- Oral Language Development*
- Ongoing Assessment*

** Additions to* Reading First *components*

Different skills and activities will be emphasized at different stages of reading development, although all components of a comprehensive lesson are needed at all levels. At the prereading stage, alphabet knowledge, phonological awareness, and language development deserve emphasis. In the decoding stage, phonological awareness and systematic, explicit teaching of phonics, word recognition, and spelling should be the main focus along with daily practice reading simple, decodable books. Reading aloud to build vocabulary and comprehension should continue until children can read "real" books for themselves. Reading with fluency, expanding vocabulary, and deciphering longer words merit emphasis in second grade.

As children gain comfort and skill with written language, more instructional time will be devoted to comprehension at the word, sentence, and whole text levels. Programs should promote wide reading in a variety of texts and thorough discussions of text meanings. Ultimately, the best readers are those who read the most and who learn to question deeply as they read. Written responses to reading promote that kind of deep reflection.

Components Typically Emphasized at Each Grade Level

Written Expression							
ComprehensionSkills/Strategies							
Passage Fluency							
Vocabulary							
Advanced Phonics/Decoding							
Basic Phonics							
Phonological Awareness							
Grade	**K**	**1**	**2**	**3**	**4**	**5**	**6+**

Exercise #7: Identify What Component Is Addressed

Given examples of instructional routines and activities of various programs, identify which major component of reading instruction is addressed by each activity: (1) phonological awareness and letter knowledge; (2) phonics, spelling, and word study; (3) reading fluency; (4) vocabulary development; (5) reading comprehension; and (6) written composition. What processing system(s) are being exercised most obviously in each of the activities?

___ The teacher asks the students to summarize the main idea of the passage in a short paragraph.

___ In small groups, the children list as many meanings as they can think of for the word *main*.

___ Children pair up. Using timers, they time each other to see how many words they can read accurately in one minute while reading a familiar passage aloud.

___ The teacher says /f/ /l/ /ē/ and asks the students to blend the sounds.

___ The teacher points to the written word *matador* and asks how many syllables are in that word.

___ Students move three poker chips into boxes as they say the single sounds of the word /h/ /ou/ /s/ (*house*).

___ Before reading, the students browse their storybooks to predict the main content of the story and to ask questions about what they will learn.

___ The teacher tells the students that *-dge* and *-ge* both stand for /j/ at the ends of words; the students then sort a group of twenty *-ge* and *-dge* words to determine when the *-dge* spelling is used.

___ Students reread words with known phonic patterns so that they can recognize them instantly without having to sound them out laboriously.

___ Students attempt to define the word *burden* by reading this sentence: The pilgrim's burden weighed heavily on his shoulders as he ascended the steep mountain trail.

Dyslexia and Other Causes of Reading Failure

Genetic, environmental, and instructional factors all contribute to the growth of reading skill. Some children come to school without the kind of exposure to books, book language, and vocabulary that support the development of literacy. They can be called "experience-deficient" and will be the focus of discussion in the modules on vocabulary and oral language development. Some students have generally weak verbal abilities in all areas. An increasing number of students are learning English as a second language. Some children fall behind, even though they are capable of learning, simply because their instruction has been insufficient. And some have legitimate, biologically based learning disabilities that deserve to be properly assessed, classified, and treated through special education and related services.

What About Dyslexia?

Dyslexia is a useful term for a specific, biologically based predisposition toward a learning disorder that adversely affects the ability to read and write. Dyslexia ("difficulty with language" according to its Greek roots) is a common problem that can affect people of all IQ levels and all walks of life across a continuum of reading difficulty. It does not refer to "making reversals" or "seeing things backwards." Estimates of the prevalence of intrinsic or biologically based reading disabilities vary from 17% in the Connecticut Longitudinal Study at Yale University to 11% in an epidemiological study by the Mayo Clinic in Rochester, Minnesota. Most of these children, however, can be taught to read.

Dyslexia is currently defined by the International Dyslexia Association and the National Institutes of Child Health and Human Development as follows[12]:

> Dyslexia is a specific learning disability that is neurobiological in origin. It is characterized by difficulties with accurate and/or fluent word recognition and by poor spelling and decoding abilities. These difficulties typically result from a deficit in the phonological component of language that is often unexpected in relation to other cognitive abilities and the provision of effective classroom instruction. Secondary consequences may include problems in reading comprehension and reduced reading experience that can impede growth of vocabulary and background knowledge.

12 Lyon, Shaywitz, & Shaywitz, 2003.

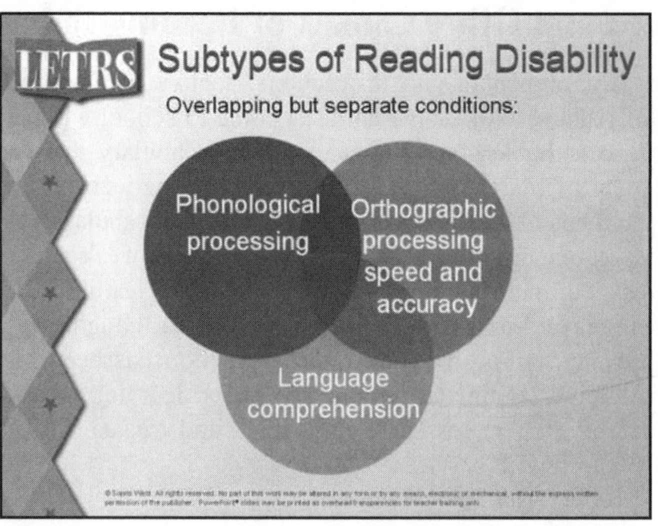

Slide 39

Progress has been made in understanding all types of reading disabilities. Among the children with developmental reading disabilities, about 90% have trouble with accurate and fluent word recognition usually related to a phonological processing deficit. Children who cannot read words well also have trouble with comprehension. A subgroup of those children, however, estimated by some researchers to be about 10%, appear to be accurate but too slow in word recognition; they have specific weaknesses with *speed* of word recognition and reading fluency, although they do relatively well on tests of phoneme awareness and other phonological skills. Some (about 10% of poor readers) appear to decode words better than they can comprehend the meanings of passages. Thus, researchers currently propose that there are three kinds of developmental reading disabilities that often overlap but can be separate and distinct:

1. Phonological deficit, implicating a core problem in the phonological processing system of oral language

2. Orthographic processing deficit, affecting speed and accuracy of printed word recognition, also called a naming speed or fluency problem

3. Comprehension deficit, often coinciding with the first two types of problems, but specifically found in children with social-linguistic disabilities (autism spectrum), vocabulary weaknesses, generalized language learning disorders, and learning difficulties affecting abstract reasoning and logical thinking

Related and overlapping problems often include pencil grip and letter formation, sustained attention to task, anxiety, task avoidance, impulse control, distractibility, comprehension of spoken language, and mathematical calculation.

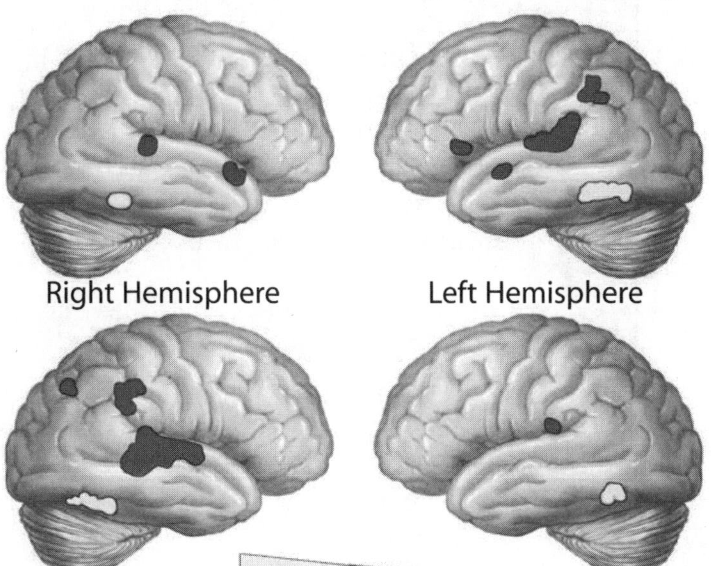

Provided by Dr. Jack Fletcher, University of Texas-Houston Health Science Center.

Dyslexic children have been shown on functional magnetic resonance imaging studies to activate different brain regions from normally progressing students of the same age. For example, they employ parts of the brain in the right hemisphere that are not activated by normal readers. The left hemisphere regions activated by normally progressing readers are underactivated in the dyslexic—that is, until intensive and effective remediation has occurred.[13] Several studies have now shown that dyslexic students' brain activation patterns can be "normalized" if remediation is early, intensive, and effectively designed.

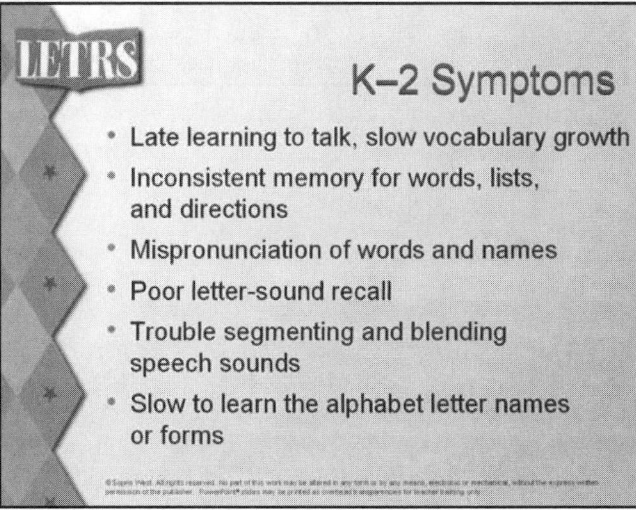

Slide 40

[13] For much more detail on neurological studies of dyslexia, see S. Shaywitz (2003).

Grades 3–4 Symptoms

- Reads too slowly, word by word
- Misreads the same words over and over
- Can't spell common words, certain speech sound sequences, or common syllable patterns

Slide 41

Grades 5–8 Symptoms

- Continues to be a slow reader
- Vocabulary is not growing at expected rate
- Spells phonetically, misspells common words
- Miscomprehends complex sentences, figures of speech, subtle inferences
- Has trouble learning foreign languages
- Writing is sparse and disorganized

Slide 42

Exercise #8: Discussion of Work Samples From Children With Reading Problems

View the following examples of the work of students who are functioning below grade level. Find evidence of phonological, orthographic, vocabulary, and/or language production difficulties.

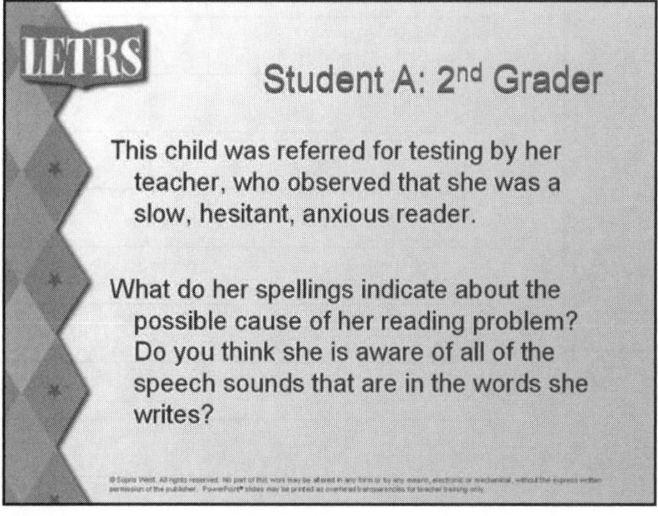

Slide 43

	Student spelling	Target word
1.	bed siup daf	bed ship drive
2.	bap	bump
3.	wine	when
4.	teran	train
5.	clost	closet
6.	cane	chase
7.	flot	float
8.	begs	beaches
9.	peroego	preparing
10.	pare	popping
11.	cart	cattle

Student A: 2nd Grader

Student B: 2nd Grader

This child had been receiving extra help in reading from a reading teacher.

Her reading rate was extremely slow – about 40 words per minute at the end of 2nd grade.

- Is she hearing all the sounds in words?
- What does she seem to have the most trouble remembering?

Slide 44

goo	(go)
ann	(and)
yel	(will)
hme	(him)
coc	(cook)
lot	(light)
jrs	(dress)
reh	(reach)
ntr	(enter)

Student B: 2nd Grader

LETRS

Student C: 2nd Grader

This student was asked to write about making breakfast for a friend.

He writes the sounds in words and remembers some sight words.

With what aspects of language does he appear to need the most help?

Slide 45

I makeBaken egg Chese
I use Chese surp Baken
eggs . I will Bern the eggs.
I put the gres inth pan
then put the Baken inthepan.
I put the Beter inthe pan
and Chop the egg

Student C: 2nd Grader

Summary

Reading instruction informed by research can help all children become better readers and writers, and can make a critical difference for the large number of children at risk for academic failure. Up to 40% of young children nationwide are not proficient readers, and up to two-thirds of poor, minority children fail to acquire the reading skills that open the door to scholastic success. Informed instruction applies principles and strategies that are proven to be effective and that are theoretically sound. Skilled teachers can prevent reading failure in all but a small percentage of children who are affected by chronic, severe learning disabilities.

Reading is an acquired skill for which the brain is not biologically adapted. Learning to speak is natural; human speech develops in a natural progression. Reading is not natural, requires teaching to master, and is not mastered by many who struggle with written language. Multiple neural networks must function simultaneously and automatically to support fluent reading for meaning. Among these are the phonological processor, the orthographic processor, the meaning processor, and the context processor. Each processing system plays a vital but unique role in word recognition and comprehension. Each processing system can be inefficient or weak and cause poor reading. Each processing system can be systematically addressed in reading lessons that explicate the sound system, the print system, word and phrase meanings, and the language in which they are embedded.

The demands of reading change as children acquire reading skill. Understanding the progression of reading development is essential for interpreting assessments and planning instruction. At the kindergarten level, children need to acquire phoneme awareness, letter knowledge, and the alphabetic principle in the spelling system. Oral language expansion to support future reading comprehension is also essential. First graders need to acquire the habit of sounding words out and using context clues as a backup for word recognition. Second graders consolidate their ability to decode longer words and learn to manage lengthier discourse. Third graders pick up reading speed and accuracy, typically reading about 120 words per minute by the end of that grade. At this point, the curriculum demands change. Fourth graders are expected to engage in wide reading so that they expand their vocabularies by 1,000 to 3,000 words per year. Mastery of a range of comprehension strategies is expected, including the ability to summarize, question, predict, and clarify by rereading or seeking outside information. Writing in response to reading becomes a major vehicle for developing the habit of mining a text for meaning.

The components of reading instruction remain stable throughout these stages but the emphasis in instruction will change according to the students' needs. Each well-taught lesson will give students opportunities to study language structure at various levels, expand word meanings, and employ comprehension strategies in guided oral reading. They will also apply skills to independent work, including spelling and writing.

Even under optimal conditions, some students have difficulty learning to read. Students with specific reading disabilities are most often dyslexic, in that the phonological processing demands of reading exceed their natural abilities. They remain slow and inaccurate at reading, spelling, and writing. Their problem is not a function of general intelligence, but rather a function of a specialized and acquired linguistic ability. Reading problems are independent of intellectual ability. A subgroup of poor readers is good at sounding words out but is unable to develop satisfactory speed or fluency in reading. Another small subgroup can read the words but is specifically limited in comprehension ability. Many children have problems with accuracy, speed, and comprehension.

Many other students come to reading with inadequate preparation and experience with language and books. Reading is difficult because they are unfamiliar with books and do not know the vocabulary or language patterns of written text. These students are not learning disabled and, for the most part, can be taught successfully with comprehensive, intensive, informed instruction that begins from the day they enter school.

Exercise #9: Concluding Reflections

Summarize any new insights you have gained so far about the challenges your students may face in learning to read.

LETRS

Final Summary Exercise

- What insights about learning to read may be new for you at this point?
- What concepts were the most unfamiliar?
- Did this module contradict any of your prior beliefs?
- What aspect of reading instruction do you want to know more about?

Slide 46

Bibliography

Adams, M. (1990). *Beginning to read: Learning and thinking about print*. Cambridge, MA: MIT Press.
An award-winning, readable summary of reading research up until 1990 that explains in detail the scientific basis for the components of effective reading instruction.

Adams, M. (1998). The Three-Cueing System. In J. Osborn & F. Lehr (Eds.) *Literacy for all: Issues in teaching and learning*. New York: Guilford Press.

American Federation of Teachers. (1999). *Teaching reading is rocket science*. Washington, DC: AFT.
This is a proposal by the AFT to have all teacher candidates learn about the structure of language, the basics of reading psychology, the implementation of research-based practices, and the procedures of valid assessment.

Armbruster, B., Osborn, J., & Lehr, F. (2001). *Put reading first*. Washington, DC: National Institute for Literacy.
A clearly written and beautifully produced summary of the National Reading Panel's recommendations on early reading instruction, for teachers and other educators interested in applying the guidelines and requirements of the Reading First legislation. Put Reading First is distributed by the National Institute for Literacy and published by the U.S. Department of Education.

Anderson, R. C., Heibert, E. H., Scott, J. A., & Wilkinson, I. A. G. (1985). *Becoming a Nation of Readers*. Champaign, IL: University of Illinois, Center for the Study of Reading.

Bickart, T. (1998). Summary Report of *Preventing reading difficulties in young children* (National Academy of Sciences). U.S. Department of Education.
This is a layperson's version of the National Academy of Sciences' consensus report on prevention of reading failure by Snow, Burns, and Griffin, 1998.

Blachman, B. (Ed.) (1997). *Foundations of reading acquisition and dyslexia*. Mahwah, NJ: Erlbaum.
Outstanding chapters by top researchers.

Brady, S., & Moats, L. (1997). *Informed instruction for reading success*. Baltimore, MD: International Dyslexia Association.
This is a consensus statement by the International Dyslexia Associations' board of directors on the findings of reading research and the treatment of reading disabilities.

Chall, J. (1996). *Stages of reading development* (2nd ed.). Orlando, FL: Harcourt Brace.
The revision and update of Dr. Chall's 1983 classic work in which a stage theory of reading development was first proposed.

Carroll, L. (1941). *Through the looking glass and what Alice found there*. New York: The Heritage Press.

Cunningham, A. E., & Stanovich, K. (1998). What reading does for the mind. *American Educator*, *22* (1 & 2), 8–15.
Written by two of the leading researchers on the nature of reading development, this paper traces the consequences of early reading success and failure, and the changing relationships of reading, cognitive development, and linguistic processing.

Curtis, S. (1977). *Genie: A linguistic study of a modern-day "wild child."* New York: Academic Press.

Ehri, L. (1996). Development of the ability to read words. In R. Barr, M. Kamil, P. B. Mosenthal, and P. D. Pearson (Eds.) *Handbook of reading research: Volume II* (pp.383–418). Mahwah, NJ: Lawrence Erlbaum.
A classic work of scholarship by a leading experimental psychologist and a key member of the National Reading Panel; for the serious student of reading psychology, the paper summarizes 20 years of cognitive

experiments that portray the mechanisms by which word images are formed and basic reading skill is developed.

Ehri, L. C. (1997). Sight word learning in normal readers and dyslexics. In B. Blachman (Ed.), *Foundations of Reading Acquisition and Dyslexia*. Mahwah, NJ: Lawrence Erlbaum.

Fletcher, J. M., & Lyon, G. R. (1998). Reading: A research-based approach. In W. Evers (Ed.). *What's gone wrong in America's classrooms*. Stanford, CA: Hoover Institution Press.
A summary of the NICHD reading research program and its key findings, written for the layperson.

Foorman, B. R., Francis, D. J., Shaywitz, S. E., Shaywitz, B. A., & Fletcher, J. M. (1997). The case for early reading intervention. In B. Blachman (Ed.), *Foundations of reading acquisition and dyslexia: Implications for early intervention*. Baltimore: Paul Brookes Publishing.

Foorman, B. F. (Ed.) (2003) *Preventing and remediating reading difficulties: Bringing science to scale.* Baltimore, MD: York Press.
Includes many articles by eminent reading researchers that contain readable summaries of their work to date on early reading development, early screening, early intervention, and effective instruction for older students with reading difficulties.

Gaskins, I., Ehri, L., Cress, C., O'Hara, C., & Donnelly, K. (1996). Procedures for word learning: Making discoveries about words. *The Reading Teacher*, *50*, 312–327.

Hodgson, B. (1995). *The World of Baby Animals*. N.p.: Hugh Lauter Levin Associates.

Kuhl, P., Williams, K., Lacerda, F., Stevens, K., & Lindblom, B. (1992). Linguistic experience alters phonetic perception in infants by 6 months of age. *Science*, *255*, 606–608.

Learning First Alliance. (1998). *Every child reading: An action plan.* Washington, DC: Learning First Alliance.
A consensus report from twelve educational leadership organizations on scientifically based early reading instruction.

Learning First Alliance. (2000). *Every child reading: A professional development guide*. Washington, DC: Learning First Alliance.
A consensus report from twelve educational leadership organizations on the implications of scientifically based early reading instruction for the professional development of teachers that discusses the context, content, and process of training teachers.

Liberman, A. M. (1999). The reading researcher and the reading teacher need the right theory of speech. *Scientific Studies of Reading*, *3*, 95–111.

Lyon, R., Shaywitz, S., & Shaywitz, D. (2003). A definition of dyslexia. *Annals of Dyslexia*, *53*, 1–14.

National Assessment of Educational Progress. Washington, D.C.: National Center for Education Statistics.
NAEP assessments are conducted every two years and results are posted on the NCES Web site.

National Institute of Child Health and Human Development. (2000). *Report of the National Reading Panel: An evidence-based assessment of the scientific research literature on reading and its implications for reading instruction*. Washington, DC: NICHD.
The lengthier report and its summary can be obtained from the Web site www.nationalreadingpanel.org; this is the work of a blue-ribbon panel that reviewed scientifically credible reading research, meta-analyzed the findings regarding the instruction of the components of reading, and issued recommendations that form the basis of the Reading First legislation.

National Reading Panel. (2000). *Teaching children to read: An evidence-based assessment of the scientific research literature on reading and its implications for reading instruction.* Washington, DC: National Institute of Child Health and Human Development.

Pressley, M. (1998). *Reading instruction that works.* New York: Guilford.

Rayner, K., & Pollatschek, A. (1989). *The psychology of reading.* Englewood Cliffs, NJ: Prentice-Hall.

Rayner, K., Foorman, B. F., Perfetti, C. A., Pesetsky, D., & Seidenberg, M. S. (2001). How Psychological Science Informs the Teaching of Reading. *Psychological Science in the Public Interest, 2* (2).

Rayner, K., Foorman, B. F., Perfetti, C. A., Pesetsky, D., & Seidenberg, M. S. (2002). How should reading be taught? *Scientific American, 286* (3), 84–91.
A shorter version of a lengthy monograph that appeared in *Psychological Science in the Public Interest* in November of 2001 that provides a current, scholarly, but readable review by five leading researchers in reading acquisition and reading instruction.

Seidenberg, M. S., & McClelland, J. L. (1989). A distributed, developmental model of word recognition and naming. *Pyschological Review, 96,* 523–568.

Share, D. L., & Stanovich, K. E. (1995). Cognitive processes in early reading development: Accommodating individual differences into a mode of acquisition. *Issues in Education: Contributions From Educational Psychology, 1,* 1–57.

Shaywitz, S. E. (1996). Dyslexia. *Scientific American, 275,* 98–104.
A readable summary of the contributions of functional magnetic resonance imaging and other advanced technologies to understanding the brain functions associated with reading abilities, the nature of reading disability, and the combined influences of biology and experience on brain development.

Shaywitz, S. E. (2003). *Overcoming dyslexia: A new and complete science-based program for reading problems at any level.* New York: Alfred Knopf.
A readable but comprehensive summary of the most recent neurological, genetic, and cognitive developmental and educational research on reading disabilities by a member of the National Reading Panel who directs the Yale University Center on Learning Disorders.

Snow, C. E., Burns, M. S., & Griffin, P. (1998). *Preventing reading difficulties in young children.* Washington, DC: National Academy Press.

Truffaut, F. *The Wild Child.* Film based on: Roger Shattuck (1980). The forbidden experiment: *The story of the wild boy of Aveyron.* New York: Washington Square Press.

White, E. B. (1973). *Stuart Little.* N.p.: Harper & Row.

Teacher Participant Pages–Exercise #4

Sound-Symbol Set I:

ɪ ŋ θ n f k š

ænd ə ðə wʌz

Reading words and phrases:

1. θɪn, θɪŋ, fɪš, fɪn, šɪn, θɪk
2. kɪn, kɪŋ, kɪŋk, ɪŋk, fɪšɪŋ, θɪnɪŋ
3. θɪk šɪn, θɪk ænd θɪn, θɪŋk θɪn
4. θɪŋk ɪn ɪŋk, θɪn šɪn

Reading sentences:

1. ðə kɪŋ wʌz fɪšɪŋ.
2. ðə kɪŋ wʌz θɪn.
3. ðə fɪš fɪn wʌz θɪn.
4. wʌz ðə θɪŋ ə fɪš?

Sound-Symbol Set 2:

ɔ w t

aj tu ju

Reading words:

1. θɔt, tɔt, fɔt, kɔt
2. θɔŋ, θɔt, kɔŋ, kɔf
3. ɔn, ɔf, tɔŋ, tɔk, wɔnt
4. wɔk, wɪš, wɪn, wɪθ, wɪkɪŋ

Reading phrases and sentences:

1. θɪŋk, tɔk, ænd wɔk
2. wɔnt ænd wɪš
3. θɪŋk ðə θɔt
4. tɔkɪŋ ɔn ænd ɔn
5. ðə kɪŋ kɔt ə kɔf.
6. kɪŋ kɔŋ fɔt ɔf ðə θɪŋ.
7. aj wɔnt tu fɪš wɪθ ju.
8. ju wɔkt θɪŋkɪŋ θɔts ɔn ænd ɔf.

Sound-symbol Set 3:

ʌ m s

<u>ʌv</u>

Reading words:

1. ɔsʌm, sɔs, sʌm, ʌs
2. mʌs, fʌs, mʌš, θʌm
3. sʌŋk, twɪst, twɪn, fʌŋk

Reading phrases and sentences:

1. twɪn tɔk
2. mʌš <u>ænd</u> mʌk
3. kɪŋ kɔŋ wʌz ɔsʌm.
4. <u>aj</u> wɔnt sʌmθɪŋ wɪθ sɔs.
5. aj wɔnt <u>ə</u> θʌm twɪst wɪθ fɪš.
6. sʌm ʌv ʌs wɔnt tu wɔk wɪθ <u>ju</u>.

Responses to dictation:

Cut out these symbol cards so that you can manipulate them, or make your own by copying the symbols onto sticky notes.

θ	ʌ	ŋ
ɪ	š	s
ɔ	k	f
t	w	m
n		

Cut out these sight word cards so you can manipulate them, or make your own by copying the words onto sticky notes.

ðə	wʌz	ænd
ə	aj	tu
ju	ʌv	

LETRS
Language Essentials
for Teachers of
Reading and
Spelling

Glossary

Glossary

Advanced concepts are indicated with an asterisk (*).

***AAVE:** African American vernacular English, also called Ebonics or Black English; a dialect with phonological, semantic, and syntactic features that originated with the African languages brought to the Americas by slaves

affix: a morpheme or a meaningful part of a word that is attached before or after a root to modify its meaning; a category that includes prefixes, suffixes, and infixes

***affricate:** a speech sound with features of both a fricative and a stop; in English, /ch/ and /j/ are affricates

***affrication:** the pronunciation of /t/ as /ch/ in words such as nature, and /d/ as /j/ in words such as educate

alphabetic principle: the principle that letters are used to represent individual phonemes in the spoken word; a critical insight for beginning reading and spelling

alphabetic writing system: a system of symbols that represent each consonant and vowel sound in a language

Anglo-Saxon: Old English, a Germanic language spoken in Britain before the invasion of the Norman French in 1066

base word: a free morpheme, usually of Anglo-Saxon origin, to which affixes can be added

***bound morpheme:** a meaningful part of a word that makes words only in combination with other morphemes; includes inflections, roots, prefixes, and derivational suffixes

chunk: a group of letters, processed as a unit, that corresponds to a piece of a word, usually a consonant cluster, rime pattern, syllable, or morpheme

closed sound: a consonant sound made by using the tongue, teeth, or lips to obstruct the air as it is pushed through the vocal cavity

closed syllable: a written syllable containing a single vowel letter that ends in one or more consonants; the vowel sound is short

cluster: adjacent consonants that appear before or after a vowel; a consonant blend

***coarticulation:** speaking phonemes together so that the features of each spreads to neighboring phonemes and all the segments are joined into one linguistic unit (a syllable)

concept: an idea that links other facts, words, and ideas together into a coherent whole

consonant: a phoneme (speech sound) that is not a vowel and that is formed by obstructing the flow of air with the teeth, lips, or tongue; also called a closed sound in some instructional programs; English has 25 consonant phonemes

consonant cluster: see cluster

consonant digraph: a two-letter combination that represents one speech sound that is not represented by either letter alone

consonant-le syllable: a written syllable found at the ends of words such as dawdle, single, and rubble

context: the language that surrounds a given word or phrase (linguistic context), or the field of meaningful associations that surrounds a given word or phrase (experiential context)

context processor: the neural networks that bring background knowledge and discourse to bear as word meanings are processed

cumulative instruction: teaching that proceeds in additive steps, building on what was previously taught

decodable text: text in which a high proportion of words (70 to 90%) comprise sound-symbol relationships that have already been taught; used to provide practice with specific decoding skills; a bridge between learning phonics and the application of phonics in independent reading of text

decoding: the ability to translate a word from print to speech, usually by employing knowledge of sound-symbol correspondences; also the act of deciphering a new word by sounding it out

***deep alphabetic orthography:** a writing system that represents both phonemes and morphemes

***derivational suffix:** a type of bound morpheme; a suffix—such as –ity, -ive, and -ly— that can change the part of speech of the root or base word to which it is added

dialects: mutually intelligible versions of the same language with systematic differences in phonology, word use, and/or grammatical rules

digraph: a two-letter combination that stands for a single phoneme in which neither letter represents its usual sound (ex. th, ph)

diphthong: a vowel produced by the tongue shifting position during articulation; a vowel that has a glide; a vowel that feels as if it has two parts, especially the vowels spelled ou and oi; some linguistics texts also classify all tense (long) vowels as diphthongs

direct instruction: instruction in which the teacher defines and teaches a concept, guides children through its application, and arranges for extended guided practice until mastery is achieved

dyslexia: an impairment of reading accuracy and fluency attributable to an underlying phonological deficit (see complete definition in Module 1)

***encoding:** producing written symbols for spoken language; also, spelling by sounding out

***flap:** the tongue rising behind the teeth to produce a diminished /t/ or /d/ in the middle of words such as water, better, little, and rudder

***fricative:** a consonant sound created by forcing air through a narrow opening in the vocal tract; includes /f/, /v/, /s/, /z/, /sh/, /zh/, and /th/.

generalization: a pattern in the spelling system that applies to a substantial family of words

***glide:** a type of speech sound that glides immediately into a vowel; includes /y/, /w/, and /h/

grapheme: a letter or letter combination that spells a phoneme; can be one, two, three, or four letters in English (ex. e, ei, igh, eigh)

inflection: a type of bound morpheme; a grammatical ending that does not change the part of speech of a word but that marks its tense, number, or degree in English (ex. -ed, -s, -ing)

integrated: lesson components that are interwoven and flow smoothly together

***lexicon:** name for the mental dictionary in every person's linguistic processing system

***liquid:** the speech sounds /l/ and /r/ that have vowel-like qualities and no easily definable point of articulation

logographic: a form of writing that represents the meaning of words and concepts with pictures or signs; contrasts with writing systems that represent speech sounds

long-term memory: the memory system that stores information beyond 24 hours

***marker:** in linguistics, a letter that has no sound of its own but that indicates the sound of another letter or letter combination, such as the u in the word guard that makes the /g/ a hard sound

meaning processor: the neural networks that attach meanings to words that have been heard or decoded

***metalinguistic awareness:** an acquired level of awareness of language structure and function that allows us to reflect on and consciously manipulate the language we use

Middle English: the form of English spoken between about 1200 and 1600—after the Norman invasion of England and before the time of Shakespeare

***monosyllabic:** having one syllable

morpheme: the smallest meaningful unit of the language; it may be a word or part of a word; it may be one or more syllables, as in un-inter-rupt-able

morphology: the study of the meaningful units in the language and how they are combined in word formation

***morphophonemic:** having to do with both sound and meaning

multisyllabic: having more than one syllable

narrative: text that tells about sequences of events, usually with the structure of a fiction or nonfiction story; often contrasted with expository text that reports factual information and the relationships among ideas

onset-rime: the natural division of a syllable into two parts, the onset coming before the vowel and the rime including the vowel and what follows it (ex. pl-an, shr-ill)

orthographic processor: the neural networks responsible for perceiving, storing, and retrieving the letter sequences in words

orthography: a writing system for representing language

phoneme: a speech sound that combines with others in a language system to make words; English has 40 to 44 phonemes according to various linguists

phoneme awareness (also, phonemic awareness): the conscious awareness that words are made up of segments of our own speech that are represented with letters in an alphabetic orthography

phonics: the study of the relationships between letters and the sounds they represent; also used as a descriptor for code-based instruction in reading, i.e. "the phonics approach" or "phonic reading"

phonological awareness: meta-linguistic awareness of all levels of the speech sound system, including word boundaries, stress patterns, syllables, onset-rime units, and phonemes; a more encompassing term than phoneme awareness

phonological processor: a neural network in the frontal and temporal areas of the brain, usually the left cerebral hemisphere, that is specialized for speech sound perception, memory, retrieval, and pronunciation

phonological working memory: the "online" memory system that remembers speech long enough to extract meaning from it, or that holds onto words during writing; a function of the phonological processor

phonology: the rule system within a language by which phonemes can be sequenced, combined, and pronounced to make words

***pragmatics:** the system of rules and conventions for using language and related gestures in a social context

prefix: a morpheme that precedes a root and that contributes to or modifies the meaning of a word; a common linguistic unit in Latin-based words

reading fluency: the speed of reading; the ability to read text with sufficient speed to support comprehension

root: a bound morpheme, usually of Latin origin, that cannot stand alone but that is used to form a family of words with related meanings

schwa: the "empty" vowel in an unaccented syllable, such as the last syllables of circus and bagel

semantics: the study of word and phrase meanings and relationships

***shallow alphabetic orthography:** a writing system that represents speech sounds with letters directly and consistently, using one letter for each sound

silent letter spelling: a consonant grapheme with a silent letter and a letter that corresponds to the vocalized sound, such as kn, wr, and gn

sound-symbol correspondence: same as phoneme-grapheme correspondence; the rules and patterns by which letters and letter combinations represent speech sounds

stop: a type of consonant that is spoken with one push of breath and not continued or carried out, including /p/, /b/, /t/, /d/, /k/,and /g/

structural analysis: the study of affixes, base words, and roots

suffix: a derivational morpheme (added to a root or base) that often changes the word's part of speech and modifies its meaning

***syllabic consonants:** /m/, /n/, /l/, and /r/ can do the job of a vowel and make an unaccented syllable at the ends of words such as rhythm, mitten, little, and letter

syllable: the unit of pronunciation that is organized around a vowel; it may or may not have consonants before or after the vowel

vowel: one of a set of 15 vowel phonemes in English, not including vowel-r combinations; an open phoneme that is the nucleus of every syllable; classified by tongue position and height (high to low, front to back)

whole language: a philosophy of reading instruction that de-emphasizes the importance of phonics and phonology and that emphasizes the importance of learning to recognize words as wholes through encounters in meaningful contexts

word recognition: the instant recognition of a whole word in print

Appendix A

Answers to Applicable Exercises

Module 1

Exercise #2: Comparison of Spoken and Written Language

Compare some of the characteristics of spoken language and written language; refer to the previous excerpts to note the special qualities of written language.

	Spoken	Written
Speech Sounds	Phonemes exist only as abstractions. There are no detached phoneme segments in spoken language. We may not even be conscious of the inventory of phonemes that we use. Sounds are articulated together in one unbroken auditory-verbal stream that must be processed in working memory. Sound segmentation is a learned behavior that enables us to read an alphabet.	Sounds are represented by alphabet letters, which are discrete units. Letters must be matched with sounds and must be sequentially processed, left to right, in space as well as time. Subtle speech sound variation is not represented in print, for example the affrication of /t/ (/ch/ sound) in *train* and *infatuate*.
Vocabulary	The conversation of educated adults has fewer rare words in it than the language in well-written children's books. See Cunningham and Stanovich (1998).	Compared to spoken language, written text has thousands more unusual words, figures of speech, and formalities. It contains an academic language that must be learned through schooling.
Sentence Structure	Sentences tend to be incomplete, run-on, or otherwise ungrammatical in conversational speech.	Sentences tend to be longer and more complex, with more embedded clauses and more formalities. Writers must express ideas with precision because the reader cannot ask the writer for clarification beyond what is already written down.
Paragraphs	Paragraph structures are usually not respected in oral language exchanges.	Paragraph structure is unique to written text. Cohesive devices such as linking words, appositives, repeated phrases, and pronoun referents are used deliberately to make text "hang together." Different paragraph organizations serve specific goals of logic.
Overall Structure	Conversational speech and oral language do not use the same organizational structures or conventions that are found in written text. Conversation tends to meander around a topic.	Knowledge of genre—that is the structures and conventions of narrative, expository, and poetic text—are necessary for reading and writing with understanding.
Available Context	The speaker continuously checks for understanding and responds accordingly, repeating and clarifying if necessary. The speaker can support the message with tone, body language, or facial expression.	Redundancy and clarification are not possible on the spot. The words carry the message totally. There are unique requirements of both the writer, to be explicit, and the reader, to actively construct the mental model that the author intended.

Exercise #5: Which Processors Are Involved?

Read this passage about a sports event:

Although he has had mediocre results all season, Moseley pulled off a victory today in the World Moguls competition. Consequently, he secured a spot on the U.S. Olympic Moguls Ski Team. He could not have done better.

Now, select which processing system or systems [phonological processor (PP), orthographic processor (OP), meaning processor (MP), or context processor (CP)] might support each of the following activities associated with reading. Most tasks draw on more than one processing system:

1. Recognizing that the right meaning of *spot* is "a place on the team roster." PP OP <u>MP</u> <u>CP</u>
2. Noticing that the word "world" uses an unusual spelling for the /er/ sound. <u>PP</u> <u>OP</u> MP CP
3. Sounding out *mediocre* and coming up with "med-i-o-cray." <u>PP</u> <u>OP</u> MP CP
4. Sounding out *mediocre*, mispronouncing it, and correcting the pronunciation after the meaning of the word is recognized. <u>PP</u> <u>OP</u> <u>MP</u> <u>CP</u>
5. After reading the phrase *pulled off*, recognizing that it is a figure of speech and it means "accomplished in spite of the odds." PP OP <u>MP</u> <u>CP</u>
6. Looking at the word *mogul* and noticing that the spelling could be "mogle" just by syllable spelling rules. <u>PP</u> <u>OP</u> MP CP
7. Noticing that every word that ends in a /v/ sound spells it with *ve*. <u>PP</u> <u>OP</u> MP CP
8. Aurally remembering the lines of this story after hearing them read aloud several times. <u>PP</u> OP <u>MP</u> CP
9. Knowing that *consequently* means "as a consequence of." PP OP <u>MP</u> CP
10. Reading and writing words such as *all* and *off* as whole words, without thinking consciously about the individual letter-sound relationships in them. <u>PP</u> <u>OP</u> <u>MP</u> CP
11. Isolating and pronouncing the vowel sound in the word *ski*. <u>PP</u> OP MP CP
12. Figuring out that *moguls* must be a type of skiing, based on the phrase in which it is used. PP OP <u>MP</u> <u>CP</u>

Exercise #6: Describe the Child's Phase of Reading Development

Given examples of children's work, can you describe which stage of reading and spelling development each one might represent?*

Student C

In September, recalls first two-thirds of alphabet, a few names and numerals, and fills up the page with print-like letter sequences. Probably does not understand the alphabetic principle and most likely reads a few words by sight as long as they are in context.

By April, writes a very long fairy tale with excellent phonetic spelling. Shows signs of strong phonemic awareness. Knows a correspondence for each sound (brot/brought; toock/took; wich/witch; tide/tied; char/chair). Knows digraphs ch and sh; spells sounds in blends including pr and br. Uses syllabic consonant spellings in evr/ever and aftr/after; has yet to learn that each syllable must have a vowel letter. Spells the past tense inflection phonetically (savd/saved; livd/lived) as expected. Morpheme awareness will typically develop after phoneme awareness and knowledge of sound-symbol correspondence.

Student D

Although he is a 6th grader, this student spells words phonetically, often using letters to represent speech sounds without regard for orthographic patterns or word structure. Reading is dysfluent because of slow, nonautomatic decoding. The long vowel in "huge" is spelled with a single letter, and the /k/ in "sucked" and "rocky" is spelled with only a k (suked, rocy). The /j/ in "just" is spelled with a g, a letter that can also represent /j/ but not when followed by a u. Confusion of b and d, failure to capitalize the first letter of names (Mary), and invented spellings of many common sight words suggests that this child has not made the transition from phonetic reading and spelling to orthographic awareness of letter patterns within syllables. Student D has phoneme awareness but very poor orthographic awareness. Instruction must lead him through phoneme-grapheme mapping, vowel spellings, syllable patterns, morphology, and common irregular words, with an emphasis on both accuracy and fluency.

Exercise #7: Identify What Component Is Addressed

Given examples of instructional routines and activities of various programs, identify which major component of reading instruction is addressed by each activity: (1) phonological awareness and letter knowledge; (2) phonics, spelling, and word study; (3) reading fluency; (4) vocabulary development; (5) reading comprehension; and (6) written composition. What processing system(s) are being exercised most obviously in each of the activities?

<u>6</u> The teacher asks the students to summarize the main idea of the passage in a short paragraph.

<u>4</u> In small groups, the children list as many meanings as they can think of for the word *main*.

<u>3</u> Children pair up. Using timers, they time each other to see how many words they can read accurately in one minute while reading a familiar passage aloud.

<u>1</u> The teacher says /f/ /l/ /ē/ and asks the students to blend the sounds.

<u>2</u> The teacher points to the written word *matador* and asks how many syllables are in that word.

<u>1</u> Students move three poker chips into boxes as they say the single sounds of the word /h/ /ou/ /s/ (house).

<u>5</u> Before reading, the students browse their storybooks to predict the main content of the story and to ask questions about what they will learn.

<u>2</u> The teacher tells the students that *-dge* and *-ge* both stand for /j/ at the ends of words; the students then sort a group of twenty *-ge* and *-dge* words to determine when the *-dge* spelling is used.

<u>3</u> Students reread words with known phonic patterns so that they can recognize them instantly without having to sound them out laboriously.

<u>4</u> Students attempt to define the word *burden* by reading this sentence: The pilgrim's burden weighed heavily on his shoulders as he ascended the steep mountain trail.

Exercise #8: Discussion of Work Samples From Children With Reading Problems

View the following examples of the work of students who are functioning below grade level. Find evidence of phonological, orthographic, vocabulary, and/or language production difficulties.

Student A: 2nd Grader

Developmental Spelling Inventory

This child's spelling suggests that she needs help with both phonological and orthographic processing. Learning to spell will depend on her ability to hear all of the speech sounds in a word and to remember the letter sequences by which they are spelled. Child does not know any digraph spellings (ship, when, chase, beaches). In beaches, the voiceless /ch/ sound is spelled with a "g," which could stand for a voiced phoneme /j/. The /v/ in drive is replaced with a voiceless /f/, suggesting that she confuses similar speech sounds. She leaves sounds out of consonant blends (drive, bump, train, preparing). She is not secure with short vowel spellings.

Student B: 2nd Grader

Spelling Achievement Test

Spellings by this child indicate that she "hears" the phonemes in one-syllable words but does not remember or recall the correct symbols for those sounds. She is weakest in orthographic processing. She tries to spell using immature strategies; for example, she uses a letter whose name has the /w/ sound in "will" (y) and the letter whose name has the /ch/ sound in "reach" (h). She spells the first sound in "dress" exactly as it is pronounced: /j/. She spells long vowels creatively and short vowels with letters whose names are close in articulation to the sounds (will, cook, light).

Student C: 2nd Grader

Making Bacon, Eggs, Cheese

A few grammatical "glue" words are missing in the first two sentences, and the writing seems to lack fluency of expression and connections between the sentences. The writing seems to have been produced with great effort, word by word.

Appendix B

Exercise #4: Learning to Read With Novel Symbols
Guide for the Module Instructor

Exercise #4, Learning to Read With Novel Symbols

Guide for the Module Instructor—Set 1

1. [5 min] Ask teachers to cut out the symbol cards so that they can be manipulated. Alternatively, teachers can use sticky notes to write their own symbols. If you choose this option, be sure that the symbols are correctly written on the teachers' cards before proceeding. Ten consonants and three vowels are included in this exercise, as well as some "sight" words.

2. [25 min] Lead teachers through the following steps at a comfortable pace. Start slowly, with the familiar symbols.

   a. **Phoneme production and identification; sound-symbol association:** Arrange the following sound cards on an overhead, magnetic board, or pocket chart so they are easily visible.

      f k n ŋ θ š ɪ

      SAY: Class, today we are going to learn to identify and say some sounds and learn the symbols that represent them. Some symbols are familiar to you and some are unfamiliar. We will combine the sounds into words after we learn the symbols for each. Here is the first set of symbols. Do you have those symbols picked out and lined up in front of you?

      First I'll say a sound and I will see if you can identify the sound when it is present in some spoken words.

      - **SAY**: The first sound is /f / as in *funny face*. Say /f/. What is your mouth doing when it says /f/? (The top teeth are on the lower lip and the air is pushed out continuously without engaging the voice.) Now, if you hear /f/ in the word I say, you say /f/, and hold up the symbol for the sound, like this [hold up the *f* symbol]:

frankfurter	sphinx	philanderer	puff
vender	fender	save	

      - **SAY**: The next sound is /k/ as in *king's castle*. Say /k/. What is your mouth doing as you say /k/? (Tongue is in the back of the throat; sound is stopped; there is no voice.) Now say /k/ and hold up the card if you hear /k/ in a word I say:

candle	christen	quietly	grace
chaos	macho	mackerel	

      - **SAY**: The next sound is /n/. Say /n/. What is your mouth doing as you say that sound? (Pushing the air through the nose; vocalizing; the sound is continuous; the tongue is behind the teeth.) Now you say /n/ and hold up your card if you hear /n/ in the word I say:

mnemonic	winner	anesthesia	ringing
agnostic	mental	autumn	

- **SAY**: The next sound is /ŋ/. Say /ŋ/. What is your mouth doing? (Tongue is in the back of your throat; sound goes through the nose; sound is continuous; vocal cords are engaged.) Now say /ŋ/ if you hear it in the word I say, and hold up your card:

sing	ankle	single	angel
English	anguish	strange	

Note: Some audience members may put a /g/ after the /ŋ/ because of dialect. Others may be confused by the spelling of words that use the letter n for /ŋ/. Say the sound /ŋ/ is spelled two ways, with *ng* and *n*, and that it is the third nasal sound that occurs right where the /g/ is also pronounced. Don't try to correct dialect difference.

- **SAY**: The next sound is /θ/ [unvoiced /th/]. Say /θ/. How am I making that sound? (With my tongue between my teeth; by blowing air over the tongue; by turning the voicebox off.) Now you say /θ/ and hold up your card if you hear it in the word I say:

thicket	thistle	both	filter	thunder
tangle	theory	this	thread	the

Note: Many participants will not have realized that there are two "th" sounds, a voiceless and a voiced. The voiced /th/ almost always occurs at the beginning of function words such as *the*, *this*, *then*, and *that*. Fortunately both voiced and voiceless /th/ are spelled the same way in English.

- **SAY**: The next new consonant sound is /š/ (/sh/). Describe how this sound is made. (Quiet, continuous, with the lips puckered and tongue forward.) If you hear a /š/ in a word I say, hold up your card and say /š/.

mission	chagrin	sugar	push
vision	cheese	cashier	

- **SAY**: The last sound in this set is /ɪ/. Say /ɪ/. What does your mouth do when you say /ɪ/? (It's slightly open, somewhat smiley; the vocal cords are engaged; the air is not obstructed.) Now you say /ɪ/ and hold up your card if you hear it in a word I say:

itchy	innocent	crypton	nitrate
symphony	pen		

b. **Matching a symbol to a sound:**

SAY: Now, I will say a sound. Then, you repeat the sound and hold up the symbol that makes that sound. (Say the sounds in random order until each has been said two or three times.)

f k n ŋ θ š ɪ

c. **Dictating sounds for symbol writing:**

SAY: Now I will say a sound and I want you to write the symbol. Do you need help writing any of the symbols? If so, I'll show you how. (Dictate the sounds in random order. Teachers should say the sounds as they write the symbols.)

f k n ŋ θ š ɪ

d. **Blending sounds into words:** Show lines of words on the board or overhead or pocket chart.

SAY: Now we are ready to combine the sounds into words. Look at the first word. Say the sounds as I point to them, and then blend them together.

θɪn, θɪŋ, fɪš, fɪn, šɪn, θɪk
thin, thing, fish, fin, shin, thick

kɪn, kɪŋ, kɪŋk, ɪŋk, fɪšɪŋ, θɪnɪŋ
kin, king, kink, ink, fishing, thinning

Ask for a volunteer to find the printed word that means the opposite of *fat*. Ask another to find the printed word that means "the ruler of a monarchy."

e. **Make a word chain:**

SAY: Let's start with k ɪ ŋ. Make that word. Now, change k ɪ ŋ to θ ɪ ŋ. What did you do? You changed the /k/ to /θ/ and the other sounds stayed the same. Now let's change θ ɪ ŋ to θ ɪ k. Now let's change θ ɪ k to š ɪ k. Good job.

f. **Spelling with sound-symbol cards:**

SAY: Now I will say some sounds separately. You repeat them after me, select the sound cards you need, and put the sound cards together to make a word. Place the symbol cards in order as you show the sounds that I spoke. Spell the whole word again on a white board, chalkboard, or paper.

θ ɪ k	f ɪ š	k ɪ ŋ	ɪ ŋ k	f ɪ š ɪ ŋ	θ ɪ ŋ
thick	fish	king	ink	fishing	thing

g. **Memorize some sight words:**

SAY: In order to make sentences we have to learn some words by heart—by the way they look. Later we'll be learning the sounds in those words.

This word is _______. (Use in sentence.) We underline the words that don't play fair; they have to be memorized by the way they look.

<u>ænd</u> (and) <u>ə</u> (a) <u>ðə</u> (the) <u>wʌz</u> (was)

Find the word I say in your pack of sight words (*the, a, was, and, was, the, a, and*).

h. **Read phrases and sentences:**

SAY: Now read the words in these phrases and sentences as I point to them.

θɪk šɪn θɪk <u>ænd</u> θɪn θɪŋk ɪn θɪŋk ɪn θɪŋk ɪn šɪn
thick, shin, thick, and, thin, think, in, think, in, think, in, shin

<u>ðə</u> kɪŋ <u>wʌz</u> fɪšɪŋ.
The king was fishing.

<u>ðə</u> kɪŋ <u>wʌz</u> θɪn.
The king was thin.

<u>ðə</u> fɪš fɪn <u>wʌz</u> θɪn.
The fish fin was thin.

<u>wʌz</u> <u>ðə</u> θɪŋ <u>ə</u> fɪš?
Was the thing a fish?

i. **Writing phrases and sentences:** Dictate a few phrases and sentences. Teachers should say the words aloud before writing them. Circulate around the room and help people who have made errors. When teachers are finished, show the correct spellings immediately and have the class correct their own papers.

SAY: I'm going to say some phrases and sentences. You repeat what I say and then write it down on your paper. You will be correcting your own work.

θɪk šɪn	θɪk ænd θɪn	θɪŋk θɪn
thick shin	thick and thin	think thin

ðə kɪŋ wʌz fɪšɪŋ.
The king was fishing.

ðə fɪš fɪn wʌz θɪk.
The fish fin was thick.

wʌz ðə θɪŋ ə fɪš?
Was the thing a fish?

Guide for the Module Instructor—Set 2

Now, the pace picks up a bit and there is less practice provided for each sound before word reading is attempted.

1. **SAY:** Now we are ready to learn three more sounds and three more sight words. Find the cards for these sounds and add them to your working group:

   w t ɔ

2. a. **SAY:** Let's learn the new sounds.

   - The first sound is /w/ as in <u>w</u>*ater* and <u>w</u>*ent*.
   - The second sound is /t/ as in <u>t</u>*able* and <u>t</u>*eam*.
   - The third sound is /ɔ/ as in *p*<u>*aw*</u> and <u>*aw*</u>*ning*. It's a vowel, like /ɪ/. Every syllable has a vowel. You say /ɔ/ if you hear it in the word I say.

crawl	audio	cough	laugh
potter	cauterize	dog	on

   Note: There will be dialect differences in the group. Some people believe there is no difference between the pronunciation of /ɔ/ in *caught* and the "short o" in *cot*. People will have different ways of saying the vowel in *on*.

   b. **SAY:** Find the card for the sound that I say. Then write that symbol on your paper. [Say all the sounds in random order.]

   c. **SAY:** Let's blend and read some words with our old sounds and our new sounds.

   θɔt, tɔt, fɔt, kɔt,
   thought, taught, fought, caught

   θɔŋ, θɔt, kɔŋ, kɔf
   thong, thought, kong, cough

   ɔn, ɔf, tɔŋ, tɔk, wɔnt
   on, off, tong, talk, want

   wɔk, wɪš, wɪn, wɪθ, wɪkɪŋ
   walk, wish, win, with, wicking

   d. **SAY:** Make a word chain with your cards; change one sound at a time as I say the words.

   tick, talk, walk, wick, with, win, fin, fawn, fought, thought

e. **SAY:** Let's review our sight words and add some new ones. Why do we underline them? (Because they don't play fair; we can't sound them out yet.) Hold up the card for the word I say. Then mix up your cards and read the words.

<u>aj</u> (I) <u>ə</u> (a)

<u>tu</u> (to) <u>ðə</u> (the)

<u>ju</u> (you) <u>wʌz</u> (was)

<u>ænd</u> (and)

f. **SAY:** Let's read these phrases and sentences. (At this point, let the participants go ahead and read orally on their own, following their own text.)

θɪŋk, tɔk, <u>ænd</u> wɔk
think, talk, and walk
wɔnt <u>ænd</u> wɪš
want and wish
θɪŋk <u>ðə</u> θɔt
think the thought
tɔkɪŋ ɔn <u>ænd</u> ɔn
talking on and on
<u>ðə</u> kɪŋ kɔt <u>ə</u> kɔf.
The king caught a cough.
kɪŋ kɔŋ fɔt ɔf <u>ðə</u> θɪŋ.
King Kong fought off the thing.
<u>aj</u> wɔnt tu fɪš wɪθ <u>ju</u>.
I want to fish with you.
<u>ju</u> wɔkt θɪŋkɪŋ θɔts ɔn <u>ænd</u> ɔf.
You walked thinking thoughts on and off.

g. **SAY:** Write these sentences to dictation:

kɪŋ kɔŋ fɔt ɔf <u>ðə</u> θɪŋ.
King Kong fought off the thing.
<u>aj</u> wɔnt tu fɪš wɪθ <u>ju</u>.
I want to fish with you.

Guide for the Module Instructor—Set 3

Tell participants to find these cards and add them to the group. Tell them that the sounds are:

ʌ (as in *up*, *must*, and *love*)

m (as in *moth* and *man*)

s (as in *snake*, *cycle*, and *psychology*)

The new sight word is: ʌv (*of*)

Instruction in this third set may be very brief or may be eliminated if the point has been made. Just tell the group what the correspondences are and let them go ahead and try to read the text from their own written material without any additional instruction on the /ʌ/ sound. If time permits, dictate a few of the phrases and sentences.

ɔsʌm, sɔs, sʌm, ʌs
awesome, sauce, some, us

mʌs, fʌs, mʌš, θʌm
muss, fuss, mush, thumb

sʌŋk, twɪst, twɪn, fʌŋk
sunk, twist, twin, funk

twɪn tɔk
twin talk

mʌš ænd mʌk
mush and muck

kɪŋ kɔŋ wʌz ɔsʌm.
King Kong was awesome.

aj wɔnt sʌmθ ɪŋ wɪθ sɔs.
I want something with sauce.

aj wɔnt ə θʌm twɪst wɪθ fɪš.
I want a thumb twist with fish.

sʌm ʌv ʌs wɔnt tu wɔk wɪθ ju.
Some of us want to walk with you.

NOTES

NOTES